Twayne's English Authors Series

Sylvia E. Bowman, *Editor*

INDIANA UNIVERSITY

D0386143

Leslie Stephen

 142

Leslie Stephen

By DAVID D. ZINK
Lamar University

Twayne Publishers, Inc. :: New York

Copyright © 1972 by Twayne Publishers, Inc.
All Rights Reserved

Library of Congress Catalog Card Number: 76–185454

PR
5473
.S6
Z9

MANUFACTURED IN THE UNITED STATES OF AMERICA

66917

Preface

IN this study of Leslie Stephen my general purpose is a critical rather than a biographical account. I have added nothing of significance to the biographical facts of Stephen's life. Most of the basic data was accessible to his official biographer, Frederic W. Maitland, whose *Life and Letters* appeared in 1906. Such information as seemed inappropriate for a commemorative biography in Maitland's opinion was later included in Noel G. Annan's excellent study, *Leslie Stephen* (1951). The Stephen family allowed Annan the use of some materials which revealed Stephen to have been something of a trial to his second wife and children, a view which contrasted with Maitland's picture of an eminent Victorian. It is likely that henceforth only minutiae will appear to be added to Stephen's biography.

The descriptive and evaluative functions of criticism were accomplished well by Annan. But, as Maurice Cowling observed in the introduction to his *Mill and Liberalism* (1963), each generation must interpret the value systems of the past in light of its own experiences. Furthermore, Annan's work is impressionistic at points where more extensive description seemed to be indicated. For instance, Stephen's most important work, *The History of English Thought in the Eighteenth Century*, was dismissed with a general statement.

Like Annan, I have followed Stephen's career as an illustration of Victorian rationalism tempered by a fervent Evangelical morality, a career which is thus typical of many middle-class intellectuals in the period. But particularly, I have sought to show Stephen to be of that cast of mind found not only in the nineteenth century but also today. It is the type of mind which produces both the most significant human advances and the most naïvely dogmatic blunders. I find that Stephen's liberalism exemplifies the powerful tendency of all free thought to solidify into dogma, perhaps out of the human need for certainty. Ideas which first liberate may easily become repressive to those which follow. The energies consumed in the attempt to destroy the old order leave a residue of ash which quickly solidifies into a new state: the new dogma. Only exceptional minds transcend this limitation and are thus free for creative thought.

Because of its analysis of a writer who is illustrative of the Victorian rationalist sensibility, this book should contribute to an understanding of the current objections of the youth culture to what Theodore Roszak in his *The Making of a Counterculture* (1969) calls the "objective consciousness"—the twentieth century's spiritual descendant of Victorian rationalism. It is no coincidence that both types of consciousness exhibit an insensitivity to poetry, psychology, religion, and philosophic idealism, because they both developed from the same important tendency in Western thought: the exaltation of human reason to the detriment of man's emotional life.

I have also tried to suggest the intrinsic worth of Stephen's literary criticism which has sometimes been relegated to the status of a period piece. Annan himself tended to emphasize the limitations of Stephen's tastes. I have not ignored this weakness but have sought to demonstrate that, even in a figure generally thought to be dominated by the narrowness of his middle-class values, the Victorian esthetic as Stephen practiced it was capable of producing more broadly humanistic insights than is generally recognized in the twentieth century. This potential of the Victorian esthetic has understandably been ignored during recent decades of formalist criticism. Yet when literary critics begin to ask if purely literary values are enough, as did W. W. Robson in the *Times Literary Supplement* for July 26, 1963 (pp. 552–54), a broader perspective is perhaps overdue.

The progression of this book is roughly chronological. At the same time, the diversity of Stephen's interests has made desirable the imposition of another structure. During his life he stressed, variously, journalism, intellectual history, and literary criticism, a pattern reflected by my book.

DAVID D. ZINK

Beaumont, Texas
September, 1971

Acknowledgments

I FIRST wish to thank a colleague of mine, Professor George Wall, without whose assistance I should have been in heavy seas in respect to a number of philosophic questions. I am also grateful to the Research Council of Lamar University for a grant which materially assisted in the completion of this book. Too, I must thank Mrs. Janis Stout, my research assistant, for many hours of careful work. She and the Lamar library staff were most helpful.

I owe an intellectual debt to Professor Jerome Hamilton Buckley who first awakened my interest in the history of ideas, and I hope that this book is worthy of his inspiration. Finally, I must express my great appreciation to my wife, Joan, for her moral support during this project.

Contents

Chronology

1832 Leslie Stephen born in London, November 28.
1842 Enters Eton.
1848 Enters King's College, London.
1850 Leaves King's College to enter Trinity Hall, Cambridge.
1854 Bachelor of Arts, Trinity Hall; elected a Fellow of Trinity Hall.
1855 Ordained a deacon.
1856 Becomes junior tutor of Trinity Hall and also a noted rowing coach and cross-country runner.
1859 Begins serious climbing in the Alps. Elected to the Alpine Club. This activity inspired his first book of any importance.
1862 Unable to conduct services, Stephen resigns tutorship. Culmination of rationalistic tendency of Cambridge days.
1865 Moves to London to take up the career of a journalist. Settled in his agnosticism by this time.
1867 Marries one of Thackeray's daughters, Harriet Marian ("Minny").
1868 Becomes the editor of the *Alpine Journal* (until 1872). Makes first visit to America during which he meets Ralph Waldo Emerson, James Russell Lowell, Oliver Wendell Holmes, and others.
1871 *The Playground of Europe* published; Stephen begins the editorship of *The Cornhill Magazine*.
1873 His agnosticism defined in *Essays on Freethinking and Plainspeaking*.
1874 Stephen emerges as a literary critic in the first series of *Hours in a Library*, essays collected from the *Cornhill*.
1875 His wife Minny died.
1876 His most important work, the two-volume *History of English Thought in the Eighteenth Century*, appears. Second series of *Hours in a Library*.

1878 Marries Julia Jackson, the future mother of Virginia Woolf. The first of Stephen's contributions to John Morley's English Men of Letters series published (*Samuel Johnson*).

1879 Third series of *Hours in a Library*.

1880 *Alexander Pope* (English Men of Letters).

1882 Stephen resigns editorship of the *Cornhill;* assumes command of the *Dictionary of National Biography* (until 1890). *Swift* (English Men of Letters).

1889 His work on the *Dictionary of National Biography* causes his strength to begin to fail.

1893 A more moderate statement of his agnosticism appears, *An Agnostic's Apology and Other Essays*.

1894 Last of many visits to his beloved Alps.

1895 His second wife, Julia, died.

1898 First series of *Studies of a Biographer*, 2 vols.

1900 The three-volume *English Utilitarians,* sequel to *English Thought,* appears.

1902 *George Eliot* (English Men of Letters). Second series of *Studies of a Biographer*, 2 vols.

1904 Stephen's Ford lectures of 1903 are published as *English Literature and Society in the Eighteenth Century*. *Hobbes* (English Men of Letters). Stephen dies of cancer.

CHAPTER 1

Clapham to Cambridge

I N many ways, the story of Leslie Stephen's writing career epitomizes the activities of the middle-class intellectual who, to a
considerable extent, molded the character of English society
during the Victorian age. When the middle class came to power
with the passage of the Reform Bill of 1832, its intellectuals
brought two important points of view into the public affairs of
England: the Evangelical spirit and what will later be called Victorian rationalism—which included Utilitarian and Positivist
thought. Consequently, most of the intellectual activities of nineteenth-century England can be clearly understood only in relation
to these antagonistic perspectives. More particularly, Stephen's
own case demonstrates the effect of these ideas upon the development of the history of ideas and of literary criticism during the
nineteenth century.

I The Early Years

The first major influence upon Stephen's intellectual development was his family's membership in the Clapham sect, a group
within the Evangelical party of the Church of England which
had located itself at Clapham, near London. The Victorian Evangelical party had descended from those eighteenth-century followers of John Wesley who had chosen to remain within the
Church of England with the hope of achieving internal reform.
Eighteenth-century Evangelicals found themselves closer to the
spirit of Geneva than to that of Rome; and they insisted upon the
Bible as the literal Word of God, the total depravity of man,
Christ's atonement for man's sins, and the primacy of faith.

By the nineteenth century, the movement revealed a modification of Calvinism to the extent that good works had also become
important. The Clapham sect itself had reduced the emphasis on
man's depravity by stressing man's freedom to accept the grace

13

which Christ made available. The God of mercy was given as much attention as the God of justice, and the Evangelical's duty was to make his fellow men aware of God's grace. The stress put upon the individual's personal experience of grace suggests the nature of the movement to be empirical rather than rationalistic. The experience of grace—one which dramatized both the individual's own unworthiness and the mercy extended to him and which was an emotional not an intellectual experience—was the essence of the religion. In this context, intellectual arguments for the existence of God were irrelevant.

The association of the Stephen family with Clapham began with Leslie's grandfather, James Stephen (1758–1832). Early in his career James had practiced law in the West Indies, and he was shocked at the brutality with which slaves were treated. Because of this situation and his reaction to it, he secretly supplied information to William Wilberforce (1758–1833) in England for use in the latter's campaign against the slave trade. After returning to England in 1794, James openly supported Wilberforce's activities, particularly after his own election to the House of Commons. When his position on the slave trade gained him the warm sympathy of the Evangelical sect in which Wilberforce was active, he moved to Clapham to be among like-minded people. His son, Sir James Stephen (1789–1859), continued the agitation against slavery as he rose in public service. Active in colonial affairs for twenty-two years, Sir James drafted the bill for the 1833 Abolition Act, and shortly after doing so he became the under secretary of state for colonial affairs.

The environment had two principal consequences for Leslie Stephen: the empirical nature of Evangelical religion appears to have predisposed him to another empiricism which he would later espouse at Cambridge University: Utilitarianism. Second, the movement also reinforced the traditional Protestant independence. Besides the experience of conversion, the Evangelical, in a daily personal communion with his Maker, developed his own conscience, which he finally trusted as his own highest guide. The result was that the individual became habituated to independent thinking. This cast of mind received additional reinforcement as a result of membership in a set which combined intellectual vigor and values, rigorous self-criticism, and a sense of a mission to enlighten the nation. For Stephen, the result of these influences was the psychological independence necessary for a man of principle to venture into the arena of public letters and to champion controversial ideas.[1]

The impress of the Evangelical spirit was clearly ethical in Stephen's case. The qualities of his writing—its sincerity, its demonstration of a felt duty to speak one's mind regardless of consequences, the unrelenting emphasis on conduct, and the compulsion to propagate one's values—are traceable to his Evangelical upbringing. More specifically, the vital role of the Evangelical family in religious activities was to cause Stephen, as his second biographer, Noel G. Annan, has noted, to base the morality of society upon the family unit in his *Science of Ethics*.[2] On the other hand, as will be developed below in the account of Stephen's increasingly rationalistic thought, Evangelicalism was finally unsatisfactory to a mind which had no personal religious experiences to account for the larger human condition—especially for the problem of evil.

The Stephen home reflects none of the repressive austerity which we have grown accustomed to associate with the lives of other Evangelical families in the nineteenth century such as is seen in the diaries of John Ruskin or in Edmund Gosse's *Father and Son* (1907). It seems to have been a home in which Christianity was graciously inculcated by example rather than by rigid authority. Since the Evangelical movement is often considered to be hostile both to the life of the imagination and of the mind, Leslie Stephen's early familial experiences suggest a variation from the usual pattern. His mother began his Latin and French lessons when he was seven, although his physical constitution severely limited his application. His mother also encouraged a taste for poetry, and Leslie enjoyed William Wordsworth's poems at this same age. At eight, he developed a passion for Sir Walter Scott, especially for *The Lady of the Lake* and *Marmion*. For a time, he spent much of his limited physical energy in rapturous absorption, either reciting or listening to recitations of Scott and other Romantics, especially poets. Later, this enthusiasm for Wordsworth appeared in his criticism, but Scott was not to fare so well.

This childhood experience reveals a sensitivity to beauty in poetry which was so acute as to be a physical liability, for his emotional capacity was stretched beyond what his physical makeup would bear. His mother's consultation with a doctor produced a diagnosis that Leslie was tending toward the malady of the period—brain fever. School as well as sea air was prescribed, and there was to be no more poetry. Leslie entered a private school in October at Brighton where his family had just moved. His health was much improved in something over a year, although it continued to handicap him on into his Cambridge days. Whether or not this regime killed a poet to make a critic as his first biographer, F. W. Maitland, has suggested,[3] Stephen's sensitivity to poetry was certainly forced to give way henceforth to the development of other capacities.

During the following four years in a public school, Stephen's family resided in Windsor where Leslie and his brother Fitzjames were to endure the psychological and physical hazards of being day boys, never pleasant in any boarding school and apparently still less so in the nineteenth-century English public schools. The brothers entered Eton in April, 1842, and were hazed mercilessly from the beginning. Nothing in their home life had prepared them for such suffering, for they were serious-minded middle-class boys who were used to reading the Romantic poets and the Bible. Those who bullied them preferred field sports and, in addition, thought of day boys as social climbers. Fitzjames, the physically tougher of the two brothers, defended both of them with his fists.

In Stephen's memory the public-school portion of his education supplied him with both physical and mental discipline, whatever the deficiencies of the institution. Nonetheless, Stephen and other critics later identified various faults of the public schools and helped to initiate reforms. Stephen's general impression of the worth of these schools emerges twenty-seven years later in an essay in the *Cornhill Magazine.* "The average lad of eighteen who comes up to the Universities from one of our great places of education shows a negation of useful knowledge which is, in its way, a really impressive phenomenon."[4] After Leslie and Fitzjames left Eton in 1846, Leslie spent the time between Eton and Cambridge with private tutors and in attendance at King's College in London. In 1850, he entered his father's old college, Trinity Hall, at Cambridge University.

II *Cambridge Student*

At Cambridge, Stephen was finally provided an environment in which a natural instinct for leadership cultivated by his Clapham experiences could assert itself; however, his new role was not to emerge at once. For instance, as much as he would have appreciated membership in the Apostles, the Cambridge discussion group founded earlier by Tennyson, Arthur H. Hallam, and others, either his abruptness in conversation or the anti-intellectual appearance that his rowing enthusiasm gave him denied him an invitation.[5] His intellectual qualities were not to be noted, in fact, for some time. Indeed, he first asserted himself as an athlete who incidentally read. He did not row well, but he enjoyed the hearty comradeship and displayed real ability as a coach. Rowing was to be the first bridge between the serious-minded and sensitive introvert and the assertive controversialist. This role gave him the self-confidence of a successful leader, and it initiated a psychological mechanism which continued to operate during his alpine work and his weekend hikes in England. Hearty male followers in vigorous but relatively simple physical enterprises provided an important kind of satisfaction for the rest of his life.

Presenting the appearance of an undergraduate who cared nothing for the life of the mind, Stephen carved out his own intellectual arena, often apart from the curriculum. English literature had not been included in the studies of Stephen's day with the consequence that, as Stephen put it, "We read what we liked and because we liked it—the only kind of reading that is of much use according to my experience." [6] Among his Cambridge contemporaries were the enthusiastic Dickens men who defended their hero against the Thackeray men, and Stephen was one of the latter. *Vanity Fair*, which had concluded its serial appearance in 1848, was the first book which he purchased for himself. Whether or not there is a causal connection, Thackeray's interest in the eighteenth century anticipated Stephen's own. Other undergraduate cults were built around the novels of the Brontë sisters and the poetry of Tennyson and Browning. Stephen's interest in literature was not strong enough at this time to draw him into the literary set, however. He had yet as an undergraduate to overcome his introverted nature. We see him at this period as a "tall, gaunt, and shy man who read mathematics, and hovered on the edge of a conversation without boldly taking his part" (Maitland, 48).

Despite the apparent freedom of the English undergraduate—few lectures, none of them mandatory, a weekly meeting with his tutor, the rest of his time spent as he wished—an iron necessity operated. He must assume the responsibility for preparing himself for strenuous final examinations which had to be taken at the end of his three-year residence at the university. If he had professional or worldly aspirations generally, he had not only to train himself for the honors examinations but to prepare himself well enough to ensure a respectable standing (class) among the minority who took honors degrees. A first class opened all doors; a second deprived him of a chance at university appointments; a third class was meaningless.

In Stephen's day, the usual honors reading was done in mathematics or Classical studies. The highly competitive nature of the examination system, combined with the laxity of the college tutors,[7] made it necessary for ambitious students to engage private tutors, or "coaches," who would drive them to their best. Stephen, who elected mathematics, was coached by Isaac Todhunter whom Stephen still venerated late in his life for a single-minded devotion to mathematics. The pressure of meeting two or three times a week a hard-driving coach with rigorous standards like Todhunter lessened the student's responsibility only slightly. The experience provided a standard of performance for Stephen which he never forgot; as he put it, it taught him "respect for abilities and energies to which [he] . . . could make no pretence. One may fancy oneself to be a philosopher or a poet without much ground for it, but a mathematician gives such palpable proofs of his superiority that one can have no illusions as to one's own talent."[8]

Such satisfactions as were not provided by rowing, reading, and preparations for the honors examinations (the mathematical Tripos) were found in Stephen's close friendship with a radical contemporary, Henry Fawcett. Fawcett was not interested in discussions of literature. Neither did he find common cause with those who followed Carlyle or the liberal theology of F. D. Maurice. Fawcett was a political activist who preferred the simple and direct answers to problems of the human condition. He found them in the ideas of the Philosophic Radicals, the Utilitarian party which was active in the reformed Parliament under John Stuart Mill's intellectual leadership from 1832 until 1838. Whatever the final effect of this philosophy upon English politics, the Utilitarian cast of mind represented by John Stuart Mill ultimately proved a limiting factor for Stephen in his literary criticism. On the other hand, the rationalistic tendency[9] which the philosophy represented was first of use to Stephen in shaping him as a historian of ideas.

The friendship with Fawcett drew Stephen into the rough and tumble of practical politics and immediate social questions such as free trade, social equality of the sexes, and the elimination of religious tests for university entrance. Within a few years Stephen found himself temperamentally unsuited to such pursuits, and in later life he recognized a certain narrowness in Fawcett himself. At the time, however, Stephen and his friends possessed the usual undergraduate smugness about their views. Indeed, Stephen later recalled that the typical Cambridge men were then "believers in hard facts and figures, admirers of strenuous common sense, and hearty despisers of sentimentalism." Stephen admitted that these views were accompanied by a cynical pose which often degenerated into a real cynicism. He was also able to admit that such denials of feeling constituted "juvenile affectation." [10]

The philosophic bible of Stephen and Fawcett's undergraduate circle was John Stuart Mill's *System of Logic* (1843). Stephen in his *English Utilitarians* (1900) speaks of the *System of Logic* as a "sacred book for students who claimed to be genuine Liberals." [11] Whatever the fallacies of Mill's thought, he then appeared to Stephen and his contemporaries as the epitome of "pure passionless reason." [12] His work represents an attempt to revive induction which had been demolished by David Hume's empiricism. Mill's idea was a new kind of logic which would link the new social sciences to the natural sciences, the method of which he took to be essentially inductive.[13] Following Auguste Comte, the pioneer of sociology, Mill envisioned sociology as a scientific study of society which would provide both laws defining the conditions necessary for social stability and laws governing the change from one state of society to the succeeding state.

As Mill approached the problem of a sociological logic, he rejected the type of deductive reasoning represented by the syllogism. When we reason in this fashion we do not add to knowledge but simply manipulate the known. All men are mortal, Socrates is a man, therefore Socrates is mortal, is true once we accept its several definitions. Such propositions simply summarize previous inductions. Mill also noted the objection of David Hume to induction: one yet-to-be-discovered case which does not square with the previous cases renders an inductive argument invalid. But, said Mill, acceptance of Hume brings us to a foolish conclusion: science is invalid.[14] And, in an age which found itself increasingly enamored of science and what it took to be scientific methods, such a conclusion was unthinkable. Careless of the circularity of his argument and ignoring Hume again, Mill used the uniformity of Nature to validate scientific laws and then turned about to validate the uniformity of Nature with the same scientific laws. And he did so to establish the credentials of the inductive method.

As Mill approached the social sciences, however, he found that the mass of data rendered the purely inductive approach impractical. The answer was Comte's "Inverse Deductive Method." First, the sociologist should infer the empirical laws of society from a careful study of history. Next, he should, as far as possible, verify these inductions by deductions from the laws of degree of probability. For example, we may note the progressive tendency for mental faculties to dominate physical abilities as society evolves. Such an empirical law of society induced from history must then be verified by reference to the basic laws of human behavior. If it is found that the individual exhibits such an evolution, a statement about the probable truth of the empirical law of society is acceptable.

One such empirical law of society emerges which both Comte and Mill could agree on; the concept that, as the ideas and beliefs of society changed, the society changes. We may argue today that ideas are the resultants of cultural conditions rather than themselves the causal factors; Stephen was later to consider this possibility. In his *English Literature and Society in the Eighteenth Century* (1904), he reversed Mill's proposition. But for these Victorian rationalists the proposition was self-evident. Social change both followed and was caused by changes of ideas and beliefs. The two diverged when evaluating such change. Historical changes in the structure of society simply presented themselves to Mill as a sequential movement in time. Comte judged such changes to be improvement, and the latest was the best.

Comte's law of the three stages makes clear his value judgments. In the first, or theological, stage, man explains natural phenomena by supernatural agencies which intervene directly. In the second, or metaphysical, stage, his speculation accounts for such phenomena by metaphysical abstractions; and, in the third, or positive, stage, phenomena are examined to discover causal relations and similarities. This development describes for Comte the evolution of the social sciences. To put it another way, man first explained his world as the work of an anthropomorphic and providential God, then as a world of mystical forces manifested by Nature, and finally as a world of things and events in which causality, instead of a first cause, was to be discovered.

In all of his thinking Mill shared Comte's expectation of employing the historical method to frame laws from past historical events which would not only explain the present but predict the future. Such faith parallels the Victorian's confident hope that, by improving man's physical environment, science itself would bring a new age; for, at this point, technology was still regarded as an undiluted blessing. Mill's attempt to link the embryonic social sciences to the physical sciences suggested inferentially to the English reader that science was the primary source of truth. Mill can thus be seen in the role of preparing the way for a widespread English acceptance of Charles Darwin's theories of biological evolution when T. H. Huxley undertook to popularize him.

To the educated reader of Stephen's undergraduate days, Mill's *System of Logic* presented itself, as Herbert Spencer was to say, as "an authoritative embodiment and justification of the beliefs and practices of most cultivated men." [15] This work advanced an organic concept of history which functioned by discoverable natural laws, and it stressed causality, particularly the process by which circumstances generate new ideas which, in their turn, cause both social change and new historical tendencies. Readers of the *Logic* found themselves possessed of a new dogma. Science was conceived of as a series of iron laws patiently arrived at by gathering indisputable facts, as the only acceptable method for all other human investigations, and as a possibility for unifying all truth. As Stephen's actions were subsequently to prove, theology had little place in such a scheme.

III *Cambridge Don*

After Stephen became the junior tutor of Trinity Hall in 1856, his role of zealous athlete and coach continued to develop. While his contemporaries do not characterize him as an affected person, one did notice that "at times he made the most of his 'fanatical enthusiasm' for rowing" (Maitland, 72). The role served to provide him with privacy for a developing rationalistic tendency which later aligned him against many of his contemporaries. The image he presented to many was that of a reticent, aloof person. Nonetheless, to those whom he did take into his confidence, he presented a sagacious mind accompanied by warm interest in a variety of subjects; but, beyond this, as one contemporary said, he had "a warm heart that was apparent to all who knew him" (Maitland, 57).

His coaching experiences were consequently to prove the basis for strong and enduring friendships. To the young men who followed him on the river, he presented a model of selflessness in the Evangelical mode. As one student said, he "taught the Trinity undergraduate to regard himself as having been sent into the world not to lead a selfish and pampered life, but in due course to leave the world the better for his having lived in it" (Maitland, 59). Stephen himself expressed his views in this way: "I really believed that I was acting from a high sense of duty when I encouraged my pupils in rowing, and I enjoyed the supreme triumph of seeing our boat at the head of the river as much as the great victory in the mathematical tripos." [16] To those outside of his circle, such activities presented him as almost anti-intellectual. As unjust as this characterization may appear, it will finally prove to be an anticipation of a subtle but pervasive tendency of his literary criticism.

Simultaneously, another role was developing in private, one that was not to emerge until his nomination as an examiner in the moral sciences tripos in 1862. His reading had become heavily philosophical, with much attention to the Utilitarians. From Mill, he had gone on to one of Mill's enthusiasms, Comte, a thinker whose influence had been important in undergraduate discussions at the beginning of Stephen's Cambridge days. The vision of mankind moving out of the bogs of theology, leaving behind the forests of metaphysics, and emerging in the bright clearing of a brave scientific humanism where human reason would soon bring the social environment under control with the new sociology—all this held a strong appeal for the young man with an Evangelical sense of mission. He read Thomas Hobbes and the British empiricists, John Locke, George Berkeley, and Hume. Aside from Mill, the Utilitarian executors of Hume's empiricism read by Stephen during these days included Jeremy Bentham, the elder Mill, the Utilitarian historians George Grote and Henry Thomas Buckle, as well as the pioneer economists, Adam Smith and David Ricardo, whose work provided the standard texts for the Utilitarian political economists.

In addition to this reading, Stephen also read most of the milestones of the intellectual history of the period, including the German higher criticism of the Bible (including David Strauss) and Herbert Spencer. In 1862, the main consequence of this reading program presented itself when the Reverend Leslie Stephen discovered that he could no longer conduct worship services at Trinity, but the immediate effect was to confirm in him the scientific rationalism he had imbibed from reading Mill's *System of Logic.*

The conflicting roles of athlete and reader, satisfactory for a time and probably unavoidable, tended to deny Stephen opportunities for really broadening intellectual comradeship. Stephen's recollections of the intellectual climate at Cambridge are, I believe, somewhat misleading. In the following statement he correctly notes the effective preparation for a life of intellectual controversy, but the friendships he was shortly to establish in America reveal a need for other conversational ingredients: "It may be a natural illusion but it seems to me that I have never listened to better conversation than I heard on such occasions . . . in those days one could enjoy conversation in the true Johnsonian spirit, considered as a strenuous game of intellectual gymnastics, where you honored the man who fairly set his mind to yours and could give and take a 'swashing blow' with thoroughly good temper. If you did not really convert, at least you got your own opinions properly marshalled and arranged and received a valuable stimulus in elaborating your own scheme of things in general." [17]

IV *The Alps*

Meanwhile the desire for an active physical life had found another expression: Stephen had discovered the beauty and adventure of the Swiss Alps. Just after graduation he had taken a summer walking trip through the Bavarian highlands and the Tyrol. He had probably already encountered John Ruskin's praise of the Alps in *Modern Painters*, IV (1856). Ruskin's vision of the Alps consisted of admirably precise observations presented with clarity, force, and poetic imagination; and they were suffused with a moral fervor not uncongenial to Stephen. In a little essay called "In Praise of Walking," Stephen recalled that, "When long ago the Alps cast their first spell upon me, it was woven in a great degree by the eloquence of *Modern Painters*."

In the same essay Stephen admitted that there was "something earthy" in his "passion for the mountains," [18] for the physical exertion of long rapid hikes was always pleasurable to him, even in England. It was this side of his nature that found sympathy with Alfred Wills's *Wanderings in the High Alps* (1856). Wills did not have Ruskin's power of description since his style was hindered by a derivative Romantic vocabulary; but he pressed farther into the Alps and wrote stirring accounts of his ascents, including a dramatic ice climb on the Wetterhorn. These literary accounts of the beauty and the adventure of the Alps lured Stephen into them.

In 1857, when he was twenty-six, he began his first serious work on ice at Courmayeur. He quickly developed considerable ability as a climber and, while he was to prefer ice work, was also good on rock. In 1859, he was elected to the Alpine Club, which had been founded the previous year; became the president in 1865; and made in all twenty-five trips to the Alps. His list of first ascents, an impressive one, includes the Schreckhorn, Zinal Rothhorn, Mont Mallet, Bietschhorn, Lyskamm, Disgrazia, and the Blümlisalp.[19] His alpine adventures were the central fact of Stephen's life, and these first ascents place him among the pioneers of European mountaineering, a sport which was just coming to the public notice. Despite Stephen's rejection of Ruskin's concept of the Alps as temples of the Creator, climbing provided him with psychological experiences akin to the religion of his youth.

In a sense, as Noel G. Annan has suggested, Stephen's alpine experiences are in a physical sense but an extension of his rowing coach days at Cambridge. The Alps provided Stephen further physical development of the weak body of his childhood; the opportunity to express his talents for leadership in a hazardous physical undertaking; and, as will emerge later in an analysis of the *Playground of Europe,* reinforcement of these satisfactions as a result of his pleasure in the natural beauty of the mountains. As Harrison has observed, "It was Nature in all its infinite aspects that Stephen loved, not athletic feats, or 'record' time, not the dangerous glaciers and icy crags for any reason but their beauty. . . . To Stephen a climb or walk meant always the glory of the Earth, the light and air of Heaven, health, and good fellowship." [20]

The expression of this new interest had an important result: Stephen's discovery of his talent as a writer. He first appeared in 1860 as a lecturer with photographs, the next year as a translator of an insignificant German book on mountaineering, and in 1862 as the contributor of two essays to the second volume of *Peaks, Passes and Glaciers.*[21] A succession of essays published in *The Alpine Journal* were to follow, and these were to culminate in the *Playground of Europe.* The original compulsion to seek a compensatory physical life had thus produced his vocation as a writer, but it also had other effects and benefits. The many seasons in the Alps helped to offset the ennui of a winter of books in London. Demanding physical activity henceforth proved indispensable to Stephen as a foil to a life of the mind. In the next decade, his alpine expeditions were supplemented by long weekend walks in England on which Stephen led the party of his "Sunday Tramps."

Perhaps this pattern of study and exercise helps to explain the general sanity and balance of Stephen's criticism. We sometimes read criticism these days which would be the better for having been produced under similar circumstances, for criticism speaks with more authority when it suggests some sort of distinct relationship to the life of feeling which most men lead. In Stephen's own case, his rationalistic predilection for the abstractions of the world of mathematics, logical analysis, and what he took to be the scientific method had to be offset if he were to be successful as a critic of imaginative literature. Otherwise, his tendency toward emotional desiccation might have been more harmful than it

YEARY LIBRARY
LAREDO JR. COLLEGE
LAREDO, TEXAS

was; for the case of Charles Darwin illustrates the denial of an emotional life among some Victorians as a consequence of a rationalistic orientation.

In his *Autobiography* Darwin laments a loss of a taste for literature which he had enjoyed until the age of thirty. He notes that his mind had "become a kind of machine for grinding general laws out of large collections of facts," but he cannot explain why it should have destroyed his pleasure in beauty. He says that "If I had to live my life again I would make it a rule to read some poetry and listen to some music at least once a week. . . ." Under such conditions, Darwin feels that he might have preserved a sensitivity to beauty, a faculty whose loss seemed indicative to Darwin of a general diminution of feeling with a concomitant diminishing of his ethical perceptions.[22] As manifested in Stephen's intellectual life, the rationalistic tendency was to prove more helpful to him as a historian of ideas than as a critic of poetry.

V *Cambridge Agnostic*

When Stephen accepted priest's orders at Cambridge, he had taken them as a requirement for holding a university position. Aside from the role of don, the only other plausible career which had presented itself to Stephen was the law—in which he had no interest. A university career was also one which pleased Stephen's father who had hoped to have a son in the clergy. The position itself had the consequence of relieving his father's financial burden, which was of some concern at this time. Finally, Stephen had developed a warm feeling for the Cambridge life. Religious fervor is conspicuously absent from these reasons.

Stephen's transition to agnosticism was primarily an intellectual rather than an emotional development. As we have seen, his reading of Mill predisposed him to be receptive to the new sciences. Although we find no direct evidence of his having read Sir Charles Lyell's *Principles of Geology* (1830), the influence of the new geology is pervasive in Stephen's *Playground of Europe,* as will be seen below. Lyell's pioneering work laid to rest various theories of cataclysmic reshaping of the earth through direct intervention by a divinity; in their place, Lyell presented a development of the ideas of James Hutton whose uniformitarianism in his *Theory of the Earth* (1795) had earlier failed to win the support of geological specialists. As Lyell said in his recapitulation of the evolution of geology as a science,

Many appearances, which had for a long time been regarded as indicating mysterious and extraordinary agency, were finally recognized as the necessary result of the laws now governing the material world; and the discovery of this unlooked-for conformity has at length induced some philosophers to infer, that, during the ages contemplated in geology, there has never been any interruption to the agency of the same uniform laws of change. The same assemblage of general causes, they conceive, may have been sufficient to produce, by their various combinations, the endless diversity of effects, of which the shell of the earth has produced the memorials; and, consistently with these principles, the recurrence of analogous changes is expected by them in time to come.[23]

The moderate tone, indirection, and quiet authority of this passage suggest the reasons for Lyell's acceptance by many Victorians, an acceptance which would probably not have been accorded a more outspoken scientist.

In addition to uniformity of change, Lyell further noted the necessity of a vast age for the earth if change were to be accounted for by natural processes. Man's notions of the earth's age had gradually increased during the seventeenth and eighteenth centuries. In the seventeenth century, the orthodox spoke of the earth as having been created in 4004 B.C; but some tried to argue for a greater age. In 1664, Henry Power, for instance, postulated a twenty-thousand-year age for the earth. The idea of vast time was supported during the nineteenth century by the more accurate dating of sedimentary layers of the earth's crust. The discovery of evidence of paleolithic man by Boucher de Perthes at Abbeville in 1847, confirmed by English geologists in 1858, dramatically expanded both man's idea of the earth's age and the length of man's own existence upon it.

Geology presented, therefore, a physical account of the earth's history which was at odds with the dogmas of theology; and biology was soon to offer a similar explanation of man's development. Still later, anthropology continued the job begun by David Hume in the eighteenth century by examining the origins of religions themselves. For the rationalist, the inference was clear: once one understood how a religion has evolved, one may freely challenge its literal truth. In contrast, twentieth-century theological thought is more interested in the meaning of religious experience for the individual than in arguing about the literal truth of any dogma devised by man.

Besides these challenges to traditional theology, there were more direct assaults by German theologians, who were beginning to look at the Bible critically. Representative of the movement was David Strauss whose textual criticism told heavily against miracles for rationalistic readers. His *Das Leben Jesu* (1835), which reduced the biographical detail of the life of Jesus to a faint oral tradition, was translated into English by George Eliot in 1846. Such a work set the scene for Darwin's great work, *The Origin of Species* (1859), and for the controversial Bible criticism of English churchmen like Bishop Colenso in the 1860's.

This flurry of intellectual activity was recorded by Stephen, who as a don had continued a heavy reading program. The upshot was that one day in 1862 he found himself unable to conduct services any longer. His historical sense, conditioned by Mill and Comte and by German criticism, was affronted: "I had to take part in services where the story of the flood or of Joshua's staying the sun to massacre the Amorites were solemnly read as if they were authentic and edifying narratives—as true as the stories of the Lisbon earthquake or the battle of Waterloo, besides being creditable to the morality of Jehovah. It may be easy to read any meaning into a dogma, but since allegorising has gone out of fashion historical narratives are not so malleable. They were, it seemed to me, true or false, and could not be both at once."

When Stephen recorded a sense of relief upon making his decision, he attempted to explain the feeling by saying that his belief had occupied the "superficial stratum" of his thoughts instead of being associated with his "fundamental convictions." [24] As I noted previously, Stephen had, in fact, already been led to a new dogma by Mill. What he described as the loss of his faith represented, therefore, a process of facing the implications of his old and new dogmas, a process facilitated by the rationalistic methodology. Regarded in another way, the religious experience of his youth, which had involved his emotions deeply and which had paralleled his pleasure in Romantic poetry, had gradually come to assume a smaller role as Stephen developed his rationalistic bent.

One of Stephen's biographers credits Darwin's *the Origin of Species* with being the decisive intellectual influence in Stephen's loss of faith.[25] However, Stephen's agnosticism was inevitable, given the chain of ideas and attitudes set in motion by his Cambridge reading; but certain inferences from *the Origin of Species* may well have crystallized his thinking. A reader of Darwin, previously brought up on the idea of a Creation composed of fixed types of life originated by the Creator, would need to make certain adjustments when he encountered Darwin's hypothesis. The idea that variations in life forms, however introduced, must become emphasized if they were favorable to the struggle for existence, while unfavorable variations lead to extinction of the type, presented a clear challenge to an orthodox theology which based itself upon special creation. Darwin's speculation about the mechanism of variation, which involved, among other factors, crude notions of heredity and of changes in environment, stressed for Stephen and his contemporaries the idea of a chance universe rather than an ordered, purposive one.

For the Victorian rationalist interested in sociology, Darwin's hypothesis was transferred without his sanction deductively into the new social sciences in several ways. For instance, this biological hypothesis, treated as a law, validated the concept of society and its institutions as an evolving organism, thus enhancing the credentials of the historical method. Furthermore, it gave the new sociology its special concern with environment. If environment could operate to cause the extinction of a species, what about human environment? If it is not controlled, might not man face extinction? Stephen's concern with the historical method finally demonstrates that the biological concept of society had the largest appeal for him. The immediate consequence, however, would certainly have been an affirmation of the truth of science as opposed to that of theology or metaphysics. *The Origin of Species,* for Stephen, represented, then, a dramatic denouement of the tendency of his reading since entering Cambridge.

VI *Tourist in America*

After Stephen found himself unable to participate in religious services at Cambridge, he resigned his tutorship and entered an aimless period at Trinity Hall during which he examined in the moral sciences, coached his boat crew, and spent summers climbing in the Alps. The last two years at Cambridge proved increasingly frustrating to him, and consequently, he "became heartily sick of the University life" (Maitland, 143). Perhaps the most meaningful of his experiences during these years was his visit to the United States during the Civil War. In debates at Cambridge, his Claphamite hostility to slavery had brought him into conflict with supporters of the Confederacy; one of his motives for visiting America in wartime was to gather ammunition for such debates. In fact, during the visit he relayed information back to his fellow radical, Fawcett, stressing the idea that the South was bound to lose since the North had decided to prosecute the war to a successful conclusion.

During his stay in America, Stephen found himself constantly on the defensive in political discussions, for Northerners were unable to understand English sympathies for the South. They presumed that such feeling meant that the English had lost their aversion to slavery. Stephen found it difficult to convince his hosts that slavery did not present itself as the central issue to his countrymen. The supercilious attitude of the London *Times* toward both sides would have illuminated the English upper-class position on the war but would have alienated his hosts.[26] Stephen's only answer was, therefore, that Englishmen were really uninformed about both the war and American affairs in general. He found himself generally sympathetic to the nation since he largely met Northerners determined to destroy slavery.

Unlike other nineteenth-century English visitors, such as Charles Dickens and Matthew Arnold, Stephen came neither to lecture for money nor to patronize his American cousins. Letters to his mother at this time are full of praise for his new friends at Cambridge, Massachusetts; for he appreciated their literary activities and especially their inclination toward work—not, in his opinion, attributes of the Cambridge don. The person he found most congenial was James Russell Lowell who, when Stephen met him, had already established himself in American letters. At twenty-nine, Lowell had capped an already established poetic reputation with a particularly brilliant year (1848) which had included *The Biglow Papers* and *A Fable for Critics*. After a period of travel in Europe, he had accepted a professorship at Harvard (1855), and in 1857 he had become the first editor of the new *Atlantic Monthly*.

Cambridge University had not provided Stephen with the sort of vivacious and far-ranging literary conversation which he met at Lowell's pre-Revolutionary house, Elmwood. Stephen found his host to be "one of the very pleasantest men I ever met" (Maitland, 114), and the breadth of Lowell's erudition enticed Stephen into a two-day visit, followed by another week at the end of his American tour. Lowell's learning was enhanced by two qualities which endeared him to Stephen: his Down East Yankee humor and his distaste for "humbug." In fact, Stephen's visit caused his own sense of humor to be permanently imprinted with the dry and deliberate Boston approach. The affection which developed from the brief acquaintance is obvious in the letters the two ex-changed for the rest of their lives. Stephen repeated the visit to Elmwood during his 1868 trip to the United States, and Lowell enjoyed the Stephens' hospitality during his five years in London as the American minister to the Court of St. James in the 1880's.

The friendship was enhanced by values which they held in common, for both men shared the idea that literature possesses a didactic function. A corollary to this notion was the idea that certain subjects were not appropriate for literature, particularly those which encroached upon the domain of sex. They were also, in their separate ways, political radicals; they could agree, for instance, in condemning slavery. Paradoxically, their liberalism was modified by the assumption that democracy would always function most soundly when directed by educated gentlemen—which is what we would expect from a New England Brahmin and a Cambridge don.

During Stephen's New England stay, he met two others with whom he could converse on a subject which Lowell had not found congenial: agnosticism. Lowell had introduced him to Oliver Wendell Holmes who had then introduced him to his son, the future chief justice of the Supreme Court, who was at this time a young captain in the Union army home convalescing from a combat wound. In a letter Stephen characterized the younger Holmes as "very kind and wonderfully talkative, but with a good deal of sense . . ." (Maitland, 118). Three years later, Stephen introduced the younger Holmes to his beloved Alps as they climbed near Val d'Aosta.[27] And during the 1860's Stephen's letters to

Holmes frankly revealed Stephen's animus toward the Church of England, which he inexplicably berated for having deprived him of important, productive years.[28]

Late in the American visit, Stephen found another in Cambridge who shared his hostility to religion, Charles Eliot Norton. Agnosticism represents a significant theme in their extensive correspondence throughout the rest of the century. The impression which Norton received of Stephen suggests that the visitor was becoming less introverted and that the sympathy of his Cambridge hosts may have been having an effect. Eleven years later Norton described Stephen to John Ruskin in this fashion: "I wish you knew my friend Leslie Stephen,—one of the most affectionate and most honest-minded and modest of men; not to be knocked by any blow from his equipoise of sense and imaginative sympathy; a sceptic without bitterness, a thinker without pretention; muscular physically and mentally without brutality; shy, sensitive, tender, manly, looking out very straight on the world, and neither hoping, caring, nor fearing much in his life." [29]

Ten years later Stephen, for a moment overcoming his usual reticence in a letter to Norton, told him what their friendship had meant to him. Despite Stephen's many friends, Norton had proven to be one of two men with whom Stephen could freely discuss his agnostic views. Furthermore, the Englishman resented the irony of circumstances which had placed such an understanding friend on the other side of the Atlantic.

During the last week of his visit in the United States, Stephen also met Ralph Waldo Emerson and Nathaniel Hawthorne at Concord. He recorded no impression of Hawthorne, but he was disappointed in Emerson, who he felt manifested no "particular power" (Maitland, 118). He was also surprised at Emerson's admiration for Matthew Arnold, which he discovered to be general in New England. Some years later, Stephen, in the quiet of his study, developed real feeling for the Concord sage.

After a tour of America, Stephen spent something over a year at Cambridge before going down to London. His new friends in the United States were no doubt influential in his ultimate decision to become a man of letters. Certainly the satisfying visits with men who were active in literary projects was a timely experience because of his personal crisis. His agnosticism had put an end to his university prospects, and he had to look elsewhere to earn a living. As he left Cambridge in January, 1865, he noted in shorthand to himself that he had no future except literature, a career which he would pursue in London. He also said, "My faith in anything like religion has been gradually growing dimmer. I can scarcely believe that two-and-a-half years ago I was still reading prayers as a parson, and that a little more than a year ago I was preaching. I now believe in nothing to put it shortly but do not the less believe in morality. . . . I mean to live and die like a gentleman if possible" (Maitland, 144–45). Like other Victorian rationalists such as George Eliot and Frederic Harrison, Stephen, after first imbibing a firm system of values from an Evangelical childhood, coasted with the inertia of the original impetus while denying its source.

CHAPTER 2

Journalism in London

WHEN Stephen arrived in London in 1865, he found himself in the midst of a brilliant literary scene. Poets, novelists, biographers, historians, and essayists were writing on subjects ranging from politics to theology; and all manifested the creative and critical impulses of the age. Tennyson, Browning, Arnold, Dickens, Thackeray, George Eliot, Carlyle, Macaulay, and Ruskin provided the Victorian reader with a variety of fare during the year.[1] By their serial publication in the periodicals of the day, many of these writers had helped such publication to become respectable. The great Victorian novelists, for instance, often first met their audiences through the magazines which were at this time increasing in number. Serialization not only gave them a hearing; it also gave them a wider readership and a financial start. Another indication of the changing status of periodical publication[2] can be seen in the fact that contributors began increasingly to sign their work instead of appearing anonymously. The proliferation of magazines (a miscellany of criticism, fiction, essays, and poetry), reviews (critical essays), and newspapers made it easier for new writers like Stephen to get a foothold. The newcomer could make his appearance in installments, in separate essays, or in poems, and he could later collect them for separate publication.

The change from Cambridge to London was not a comfortable one for Stephen, but it was clearly a necessary one. Shortly after arrival he wrote to Lowell, "I have just torn myself up by the roots from Cambridge . . . a warm, cosy place . . . where I had been vegetating for near fifteen years in comfort. . . . I walked about in a gorgeous cap and gown, and everyone I met took off their hats to me. Now in London I find that people don't instinctively recognize me . . ." (Maitland, 158–59). But Stephen found the change stimulating; it helped to spur him to a ca-

reer of writing which, though it probably never flattered his ego
in the way that the Cambridge life had, produced lively friendships with most of the leading intellectuals of his day. He began
his professional writing from a more utilitarian consideration,
however. He needed a job.

At the outset, he recalled later, he had his "dreams of helping
to set the world right upon various philosophical, political, and
economic problems." Like his liberal contemporaries in the Victorian intellectual world, Stephen was expectant of the "speedy
advent of a democratic millennium." [3] He had inherited an Evangelical sense of mission which he immediately turned to account
in secular questions. In a letter to Holmes two years later he
noted that he was "not a prophet or a great teacher"; but, "on the
whole I abuse scoundrels and support what I believe to be right"
(Maitland, 200). The didactic note struck here later pervaded his
criticism and colored his work as a historian of ideas. From his
point of view, the identification of scoundrels was a purely intellectual and rational process: one simply brought his evidence together and destroyed those guilty of humbug. From another point
of view, however, certain values and attitudes fashionable among
his contemporaries facilitated the identification of scoundrels: a
scoundrel was sometimes simply a person who differed from his
position.[4]

London newspapers, like the magazines, were also beginning to
be more attractive to liberal intellectuals with causes to push. The
rise of the middle class to power after the reform bill of 1832 was
accompanied by a corresponding improvement of the status of
newspapers. Stephen's first connection was formed with the liberal *Saturday Review*, a weekly so acid in its denunciations of
Philistine taste that the outspoken liberal John Bright called it
"the *Saturday Reviler*." [5]

Begun in 1855, the *Saturday Review* already included a Stephen among its contributors; for Leslie's brother Fitzjames, a successful London lawyer, was among the most brilliant of its writers when Leslie arrived. Fitzjames introduced him to the editor,
John Douglas Cook, and the younger brother settled into a
weekly pattern of writing both a review and an article on some
social question of the day. Stephen so completely assimilated the
Olympian contempt of the *Saturday Review* style that, as he later
looked through the paper's files, he found himself unable to

identify his own work from internal evidence. With characteristic good humor, he later described his own work as the product of "overconfidence in my own infallibility. . . . I ranged over most branches of human knowledge, from popular metaphysics to the history of the last University boat-race." [6] Despite the brashness and pretension of speaking with an assumed authority on such a variety of topics, this experience was ideal in that it permitted Stephen to flex his mind, find his own interests, and make an important friendship as a consequence of his contributions. Among the younger writers of the staff Stephen met John Morley (1838–1923), about to become editor of the most influential liberal magazine of that day, the *Fortnightly Review*. Morley and Stephen became close friends. Both rationalists, they were to energize the English rationalist attack upon theology during the next decade.

Shortly after Stephen's arrival in London, another publication was founded. An afternoon paper, the *Pall Mall Gazette,* was started by George Smith. Fitzjames, who was also a regular contributor to the *Pall Mall Gazette,* introduced Leslie to Smith. This introduction began a cordial and important friendship for Leslie, who was soon to serve as editor of the *Cornhill* and later as the editor of the *Dictionary of National Biography,* both published by Smith. While Stephen enjoyed his work for the *Gazette,* it was like that which he did for the *Saturday Review*—a kind of writing which held no lasting appeal for him since it demanded, as he put it, a "kind of superficial omniscience." [7] The connection served, nonetheless, to broaden his acquaintance since the regular contributors also included Anthony Trollope, Matthew Arnold, and G. H. Lewes.

At the outset of his writing career, Stephen's work reflects the youthful faith in the efficacy of reason in practical politics, a faith he had imbibed from Fawcett's radicalism at Cambridge. One of Stephen's earliest published articles reveals his ambition to exert a direct influence upon the political arena. While still at Cambridge, he had published an attack upon American tariffs in *Macmillan's Magazine.*[8] Arguing for free trade, Stephen noted that American protectionists had, with their tariffs, pointlessly alienated their English cousins and had obscured what he felt to be the real cause of the Civil War—slavery. In his essay Stephen clearly assumes that it is sufficient to point out the fallacies of protective tariffs to a rational world which will listen and heed his advice.

During the 1860's Stephen had some basis for his liberal faith, for philosophical radicalism had made its mark upon society. As Stephen later phrased it, "the good old cause was triumphant. Mill had expounded its philosophy; Cobden had secured the definitive victory of its economic theories; Gladstone was coming into power to carry out the mandates of the new democracy." Stephen and his young liberal friends "represented intelligence and progress, against Tory stupidity and stagnation." But, writing in 1902, Stephen observed sadly that the millennium was not achieved after adoption of those political measures which they had advocated.

Worse, he noted that the liberalism of his day had been repudiated by the turn of the century. What had seemed at the time to be rational solutions to pressing social questions had, in their turn, generated new problems. For instance, he spoke of the liberals' pleasure over the abolition of the law on conspiracy. The immediate result was that trade unions prospered, but the following generation had to contend with the tyranny of trade unions which he described in 1902 as a factor at work to limit industrial production as a result of "levelling down workmen's energy." His generation of liberalism had viewed with alarm any increase of the state's power, a phenomenon held to be inevitable by the liberal of 1902. His most severe critique of the rationalistic liberalism of his youth concerned itself with the failure of the liberalism of that day to adjust itself to political and social complexities. Although Stephen finally continued to hope for a rational leaven in the loaf of politics, he had become well aware of the danger of theoretical positions. An idea in politics was for him "a device for saving thought. It enables you to act upon a little formula without taking the trouble to ask whether it be or not be relevant to the particular case." [9]

It took some time, however, for Stephen to evolve the perspective we have just cited. But his disengagement from practical matters of politics was not far off. On his thirty-fourth birthday in 1866 he described a continuing interest in political writing, but it was accompanied by a frustration with the outlets available to him. He felt that neither the *Saturday Review* nor the *Pall Mall Gazette* permitted him sufficient freedom of subject matter. Despite his involvement in the politics of the day, Stephen's literary interests continued to broaden. During the first year of his arrival in London, he had been elected president of the Alpine Club; and, at the end of his three-year term, be began to edit the *Alpine Journal*. First encouraged to write by his love of the Alps, Stephen now owed his first editorial experience to mountaineering. His work on a specialized journal of limited circulation provided him with a natural development toward the responsibility of a family magazine with a broad circulation which he encountered when he became the *Cornhill* editor in 1871.

Stephen's love of the Alps was to be relegated, however, to the status of a subsidiary emotion. When the Cambridge bachelor first reached London, two young ladies occupied the attentions of London matchmakers: the two Thackeray girls whose father had died in 1863. Anne Isabella and Harriet Marian Thackeray were included when Leslie, his sister, Fitzjames, and his wife enjoyed a river outing in June, 1865. In the meetings which followed at various social events, Leslie soon came to prefer Harriet, but his shyness prevented any immediate indication of the fact. One of the matchmakers, sensing Leslie's indecision, then arranged an ambush for him. During his 1866 summer vacation in Switzerland, the Thackeray girls suddenly turned up at Zermatt while Leslie was there. His bachelor defenses were shattered, but he postponed surrender. He hurried to Vienna to keep an appointment, incidentally meeting there the novelist George Meredith, who was to be one of Stephen's warmest friends in England. He finally capitulated to Harriet that December and was married the next June.

Minny, as Stephen came to call Harriet, brought much happiness into his life until her sudden death eight years later; but he had had to modify his idea of a wife as a possession. Furthermore, the marriage involved something more than the usual adjustment since Minny brought her sister Annie to live with them. Nonetheless, Stephen proved a devoted husband and was crushed by her death. The best portrait of Minny survives in the words of Leslie's sister: "She had a singular and indescribable social charm—a humorous, wayward and changeful grace, which captivated not only for the moment but for life, because its freshness was so unmistakeably the outcome of transparent sincerity. . . . She could never have been put into intellectual harness,

but there was a rare sureness and delicacy in her critical intuitions, whether as to personal or literary qualities" (Maitland,
254).

A series of events now caused a shift in Stephen's interests. His
marriage and his second trip to America in 1868 signal a withdrawal from political activism. His writing continues to be concerned with controversial subjects—his attacks on religion have
yet to appear—but his polemics begin to be directed at more abstract subjects instead of at immediate political questions. His
love of controversy expressed itself in the next decade in the
realm of the history of ideas with his *History of English Thought
in the Eighteenth Century* (1876).

This disengagement from direct involvement in politics also
permitted the development of Stephen as a literary critic. In his
student days English literature had provided him pleasurable
relief, as we have noted, from the abstract dryness of his studies
in mathematics. Writing about this kind of pleasure was a defen-
sible enough occupation, Stephen thought, as long as one had no
pretensions. He drifted casually into literary criticism as a journalist; and, as the title of his first collection of literary essays *Hours
in a Library* suggests, he regarded himself as a gentleman in his
library writing to other gentlemen of similar tastes. His diffidence
and his love of literature caused him to write much sensitive
and, at the same time, judicious and sensible criticism which
earned him the respect of his readers.

I Literary Critic: The Cornhill Magazine

Within a year of leaving Cambridge, Stephen's writings appeared in the *Cornhill*. His first essay, "American Humour," [10] pa-
tronized American authors such as Emerson, Longfellow, and
Hawthorne as "second rank" writers whose work resembled that
of extremely clever essays by undergraduates rather than the
"thorough and finished work of well-trained thinkers." The glib-
ness of Stephen's judgment is evident when we realize that Stephen had yet to study Emerson, for he had met him only in person, not in his work. In an anecdote about an American traveler
who remarked about the Alps, "I guess I passed some risin'
ground," Stephen noted, however, the understatement important
in nineteenth-century American humor. Other observations included his recognition that such understatement was probably a

reaction to the inflated rhetoric of public speeches and that
humor in America tended to be directed toward practical matters
(such as Lowell's political satire in the *Biglow Papers*) instead of
being enjoyed for its own sake. Despite Stephen's discussion of
humor as a political device in this essay, he is at least as interested
in esthetic questions. The synthesizing and interpretative functions of criticism are beginning to emerge.

When Stephen began in 1866 to write for the *Cornhill*, the publication was six years old. A family magazine, the *Cornhill* ran
two illustrated novels in serial, poems, book reviews, and essays
of general interest. At the time Stephen's first essay appeared,
Wilkie Collins and Trollope were serializing novels. Besides this
tame fare, however, Matthew Arnold, who had established himself as a rebel several years before,[11] was defending himself
against charges of injustice to his countrymen who had resented
being called Philistines. His cheeky defense included the statement that even Americans were no longer guilty of being Philistines. And Arnold's controversial "St. Paul and Protestantism"
soon appeared in the *Cornhill* in 1869. Stephen's own polemics
did not, however, appear in the *Cornhill*. His attacks on theology
and his agnosticism were printed in the *Fortnightly Review* and
in *Fraser's Magazine*. For the *Cornhill* audience in the years before he assumed its editorship, Stephen continued his literary criticism; wrote some travel pieces which, as we might expect, included articles on the Alps; and demonstrated his wit with the
"Cynic" series which comprised a dozen essays.

In 1868 a pair of *Cornhill* essays opened Stephen's career as a
literary critic. The two essays, one on Samuel Richardson and the
other on Daniel Defoe,[12] represent an early attempt in the Victorian period to salvage the literature of the previous century after
the Romantics had scuttled it for all men of sensitivity. In his defense of what proved to be his favorite period in English literature, Stephen perceived genuine feeling beneath the surface of
obsolete fashions, found even a measure of the picturesque—an
eighteenth-century esthetic concept still employed in the nineteenth century. Besides his sympathy with the Age of Reason,
several other stances emerge which later became characteristic
of his criticism. Demonstrable in these pieces is an interest in the
work as an illustration of the author's character. And, if Stephen

is to be satisfied with the work of art, he must be convinced of the moral earnestness of its creator. Stephen's abiding interest in biographical criticism follows naturally.

Stephen was not unique in his esthetic views, for the Victorian reader considered the artist as a teacher as much as an entertainer. And one's teacher should present the proper credentials in his own private life. Stephen did not, however, desire that literature preach: "a direct intention to prove that men ought not to steal or get drunk . . . is generally considered to be beside the novelist's purpose, and its introduction to be a fault of art." [13] Indirection is the approach suggested by Stephen's praise of Richardson's moral earnestness, which he noted in the novelist's concern with characters and motives.

Stephen's attitude in these essays toward verisimilitude in the novel is also characteristic. The early Puritan distrust of fiction as a kind of lie lingers on in Stephen's criticism: "It is not the object of a really good novelist, nor does it come within the legitimate means of high art in any department, to produce an actual illusion." The writer hampers himself "if he imposes upon himself the condition that his book shall be capable of being mistaken for a genuine narrative." [14] It should be remembered that Thackeray had preceded his *Vanity Fair* with an introduction of himself in the character of a showman exhibiting various of his own creations, and he thereby suggested at the outset of his novel artifice rather than the illusion of reality. English criticism was not ready at this point to suggest that the novel should present an illusion of reality; indeed, even Henry James's demands that fiction should be regarded as a serious art are some years in the future. His essay "Art of Fiction" was not to appear until 1884.

Nonetheless, Stephen commended both English novelists for those touches which bring their stories closer to life: Richardson, for his power of observation represented in his settings and his sensitivity to feminine psychology; Defoe, for his ability to achieve verisimilitude through his knack of imagining convincing details which make the lives of his characters more credible. At the same time, Stephen notes that the work of both men is limited by their personal character. Richardson's characters, for example, reflect his own moral priggishness—a shopkeeper's prudential morality; Defoe's present the limits of his own psychological insight. At the outset of his criticism, Stephen felt, therefore, that the worth of fiction derived from its psychological truth as presented by a novelist whose character a reader could admire.

These essays indicate Stephen's departure from the appreciative criticism often found during the Victorian period. His attempts to be analytic are hampered by his lack of a body of critical theory about the novel, one as yet unconstructed by Henry James and others. Hence he is unable to describe the achievements of Defoe and Richardson as pioneers in the genre of the novel. For instance, in reference to preceding fiction, he fails to realize that both these novelists in their characterization and setting had moved from the general to the particular specification by creating convincing individuals placed in particularized settings.[15] But this criticism can be leveled at any pioneer. The important thing is that, at the outset of his criticism, Stephen made the attempt to be analytic.

Something of Stephen's undergraduate love of argument for the sake of argument is evident in another group of *Cornhill* essays, those which began with "A Cynic's Apology." [16] Stephen's account of the role of the cynic in society (finally the critic) also owes an obvious debt to Arnold's analysis of the critic's utility to society.[17] The cynic was to serve as a gadfly to "prigs," to those who carried the self-esteem of the undergraduate into adult life. While the essay took a slap at Arnold's term "Philistine"—"like other nicknames, that word has degenerated in common use, till it is sometimes a mere shibboleth, employed by the genuine prig to designate all who are not prigs"—Stephen's description of the critic's task is quite similar to Arnold's. When the illusions of youth become the values of the adult, what is indicated is "treatment with some biting social acids which cynics are destined by nature to secrete." Then the cynic turns critic: "The critic's sneer . . . may do something to clear the atmosphere of cant, and to strip the prig of his inordinate affectations."

Although Stephen admitted the limited utility of the cynic's position, he insisted that it was essential: "By itself it can do nothing; but it gets rid of some of the constantly accumulating masses of humbug, and allows us at least to see things as they are." Stephen was asking for criticism to renovate society by sweeping away fakery and stupidity; Arnold emphasized smugness and complacency. The problem which they perceived was essentially the same: English society lacked forthright honesty. Stephen's approach, and it also suggests his limitation as a critic of society, was essentially more destructive in its emphasis; and he left picking up the pieces to those who came after him. In all of the cynic essays, Stephen's style is freewheeling and witty on the surface; but he is always in tenacious pursuit of the realities of English society beneath its surface appearance.

Stephen continued writing for the *Cornhill* for thirty-five years and produced a total of seventy-five essays for the magazine. In them, Stephen often appeared as a literary critic who had broadened his task to include the criticism of society; for he ranged in subject from the question of public school reform to vivisection. The largest group of the *Cornhill* essays, however, those which appeared under the series title, "Hours in a Library" (and were ultimately collected under the same title), are those of a writer concerned with more purely literary topics.

II *Apprentice Historian of Ideas:* Fraser's Magazine

Denied expression of his rationalism in the *Cornhill*, Stephen quickly took to the pages of *Fraser's Magazine*, at that time edited by J. A. Froude, the historian and biographer of Carlyle. *Fraser's* was more used to controversy than many Victorian magazines, for it had survived the crisis precipitated by publishing Carlyle's *Sartor Resartus* some thirty years before.[18] The tone of Stephen's writing in *Fraser's* is sufficiently evident in the title under which he collected half a dozen of his pieces from the magazine in 1873: *Freethinking and Plainspeaking.* Stephen had begun his overt attack upon religion.

The scientific utopia projected by Auguste Comte's Positivism offered Stephen an early topic for free thought.[19] His analysis of Comte's system appeared to be an attempt to account both for the interest of intellectuals in Comte and the hatred which the clergy evinced for him. Despite a pose of objectivity, Stephen's witty and apparently ironic description of Richard Congreve's view of Positivism suggests his own sympathies: Positivism was to be seen as an amalgam of the medieval church and science. "Take away, that is, such trifles as the belief in God, and the whole body of Catholic dogma, and the organization with a new creed would give us very nearly what we need." Like most commentators, Stephen found Positivism vitiated by its absurd organization, but about one point he was not as disturbed as John Stuart Mill. Mill, generally sympathetic to Comte, was hostile to his attempt to concentrate public opinion, to mobilize it to achieve his scientific society. Mill himself, in his *On Liberty* (1859), feared the tyranny of public opinion in a democracy.

Stephen, anticipating the modern planner of society, noted that Comte's vision of a scientific society was appealing because of the anarchy then prevalent in England. The school system was chaotic; the army was in need of reform; and both labor and capital were at war. A curious distrust of democracy emerges in Stephen's words: "Men of intellect should rule the world instead of deciding questions by counting heads." An astonishing statement from a liberal of that day!—especially in view of what liberals had done to broaden the franchise.

Stephen used other controversial topics besides Positivism as a cover from which to snipe at the Church of England and at religion itself. (This technique had evolved into a full battle plan by the time he began to write his *History of English Thought in the Eighteenth Century* [1876].) Stephen's first attack on theology had been a covert one, and it was made the year before Stephen began writing for *Fraser's*. In an essay about the High Church ritualism of the time,[20] Stephen, apparently defending the Broad Church position, seemed to be accounting for the increase in agnosticism and atheism in England. He found the ritualist preoccupation with ceremony genuine enough emotionally but unsupported by intellectually satisfying demonstrations of its authority: "we are substantially told that we are to refuse to trust our intellect, which, as the intellect means the faculty of discovering truth, comes, after more or less evasion, to asking us to believe a thing, not because it is true, but because it is pleasant." He concluded by saying that such a position had encouraged rationalism; and, because of its "intellectual dishonesty," the church was driving "the most intelligent classes into infidelity."

The quarrel between the religious liberalism of the Broad Church party and the sympathy for Catholic ritualism of the High Church party gave Stephen another opportunity to field test his rhetorical tactics. The specific occasion was an argument between Edward B. Pusey (1800–1882), one of the leaders of the Oxford Movement which, beginning in 1833, had tried to stress the compatibility of the Anglican Church with Roman

Catholicism, and Frederick Temple (1821–1902), who had written the lead essay in the controversial *Essays and Reviews*
(1860), a culmination of Broad Church thinking. Stephen's amusing account of *Essays and Reviews*[21] demonstrates his tactics:
"They were weak about the six days of creation; they had their
doubts about the flood, and Balaam's ass, and Jonah's whale.
They did not exactly deny the occurrence of supernatural inter-
ferences with the order of the world; but they tried to make the
miracles as little miraculous, and the prophecies as little pro-
phetic as possible." The result was a patched up and tottering
orthodoxy. The public had been disturbed by the essays and had
called their authors the "Seven Against Christ," but Stephen had
found their arguments so conventional from his rationalist point
of view that "no moderately clever undergraduate at either university could be shocked by their novelty."

In succeeding articles in *Fraser's*, Stephen worked out more explicitly his attack on religion. In one, he characterized the Broad
Church party as intellectually dishonest;[22] and he used its position
to demonstrate the necessity for "perfect intellectual sincerity."
The strident tone of his summation suggests the characteristic
temper in the 1870's of agnostic writing: "it is incomparably more
important that men should speak the plain unsophisticated truth
and have it spoken to them, than that they should support the
Articles, or the Church of England, or any other Church whatever."

Two years later, Stephen rounded out his agnostic position in
two essays, one of which, "Darwinism and Divinity,"[23] demonstrates the importance of Stephen's Cambridge reading of Darwin. Stephen's tactics in this essay illustrate his movement towards a style in controversy which was potentially less offensive
to the general Victorian reader than some of his previous journalism. He began by assuming what would have been the worst possibility for many Victorian readers: that Darwin's theory had been
completely victorious and that man was therefore to be thought of
as standing at the end of a sequence of life forms which had
begun with a very simple organism, had moved through higher
forms including the ape, and had finally evolved into man himself.
What are the consequences? Some shock, perhaps, based upon "a
prejudice or two derived from the Zoological Gardens," but what
else? One result was the validation of the historical method by

Darwinism. Then what? Does religion have to go? Well, morality, for instance, said Stephen, can be traced back to an animal instinct without destroying it. Religion itself is similarly "traceable to the spontaneous working of the human intellect." Religion then, was acceptable to Stephen so long as it was confined solely to man's instincts—but the concept of immortality was not. After Darwin, since most men do not want to give souls to monkeys, we cannot really give them to man, said Stephen. Moreover, immortality, when used as a reinforcement of morality, was for Stephen "as degrading as the grossest forms of materialism."

In his essay, Stephen clearly made every attempt to soothe the feelings of his readers at the same time that he quietly removed religion from the realm of the supernatural and located it in the instinctual behavior of man. The conciliatory tone of his attempt to characterize the religious experience as mere illusion for all sensible men is evident in this passage:

There is still quite as much room as ever for the loftiest dreams that visit the imaginations of saints or poets. The mode in which we express ourselves must, of course, be altered; but so long as the same instincts exist which sought gratification in the old language, we need not doubt but what they will frame a new one out of the changed materials of thought. The fact that religion exists is sufficient demonstration that men feel the need of loving each other, of elevating the future and the past above the present, and of rising above the purely sensual wants of our nature. . . .

In Stephen's mind, religion has clearly become only a name for the moral faculty.

The culminating article in the *Fraser's* series was his "A Bad Five Minutes in the Alps" [24] in which he used an alpine accident to dramatize his own credo. Hanging precariously from a slim hold above what he considered sure death several hundred feet below, he took stock of his beliefs. In sequence, he rejected the dogmas of theology, materialism, and Positivism, for none of these views possessed meaning for him in the face of death. Finally he decided that "this fag end of the game should be fairly played out, come what might and whatever reasons might be given for it." As a rhetorical device, personal experiences of this sort are compelling. When individuals tell us what they found meaningful in the face of death, we generally give them our attention. But the message is different with varying times and temperaments.[25]

This particular phase of Stephen's journalistic work both illustrates the Victorian rationalist mind in action and illuminates the path by which Stephen approached one of his most important tasks—that of historian of ideas. His rationalism had led him to agnosticism and then away from Cambridge into journalism. His Cambridge experiences in argument had given him an appreciation of the sort of approach which would compel the respect of a general audience. He first refined these techniques on a number of lesser controversies; then he attacked a central institution of English society: organized religion. His strongest feelings were operative in these attacks for the church represented to him the largest falsehood of the age. He was therefore driven to present his position clearly and forcefully with the hope of winning converts among the general reader. With his own distrust of metaphysical abstractions, he was in an excellent position to realize the necessity of being as concrete and as direct as possible. All this journalistic experience is valuable preparation, it would seem, for any historian of ideas. Although such a historian of ideas may write a partisan history, his writing at least gains life in a field where dullness is sometimes achieved by the best minds.

III *Victorian Agnostic: The* Fortnightly Review

After leaving Cambridge, Stephen's animus toward the Church of England had led him to regard it as a floating derelict which ought to be shelled and sunk to remove it as a hazard to the nation's navigation toward the perfect state; and many years would pass before he recognized any validity in the religious experience. Speaking as a Darwinian in 1901, he granted religion minimal credentials in his "Evolution and Religious Conceptions." More tolerant of religion at this point, he took it to be an imperfect manifestation of a legitimate human instinct: the moral sense. Theology was allowed to pass muster as a transient phenomenon, as a vehicle for ethical ideas.[26]

In the meantime, Stephen waged total war against the church. Sometimes he uses other subject matter as a cover for his agnostic views; sometimes his animus toward religion emerges more badly; and, as I have shown, he occasionally both states his views frankly and adopts a moderate and conciliatory tone. At this point, he seems to be casting about for the most effective literary tactics; but, finally, his arsenal against the church becomes diversified. On the one hand, he enjoyed the frankness permitted to him in the pages of the *Fortnightly Review;* on the other, he returned to a covert operation while presenting his apparently objective *History of English Thought in the Eighteenth Century.*

The *Fortnightly Review* first appeared in 1865. The brilliant group which founded it included Anthony Trollope, George Eliot, G. H. Lewes, and Walter Bagehot. In 1867 Lewes, the first editor, was succeeded by John Morley, who had known Stephen as a contributor to the *Saturday Review.* Morley's energetic leadership turned the magazine into a vital intellectual force in Victorian thought, for it was the principal outlet for those Victorian liberals who accepted the idea of progress as an article of the liberal-rationalist faith and who preached it either as disciples of Mill or as Positivists while they wrote about political, philosophical, and literary topics. The impressive list of those who wrote for the *Fortnightly* included J. S. Mill, Frederic Harrison, T. H. Huxley, Herbert Spencer, George Meredith[27], Matthew Arnold, Walter Bagehot, and in 1871 Stephen.

Under Morley's editorship (1867–82), the impact on English society of the rationalistic critique of traditional beliefs and values presented in the magazine was comparable to the effect on French thought of the *Encyclopaedia* (1751–65)—except, however, that no revolution ensued.[28] The *Fortnightly* spirit is clearly observed in Morley's characterization of the England of his day as

. . . a community where political forms, from the monarch down to the popular chamber, are mainly hollow shams disguising the coarse supremacy of wealth, where religion is mainly official and political, and is ever ready to dissever itself alike from the spirit of justice, the spirit of charity, and the spirit of truth, and where literature does not as a rule permit itself to discuss serious subjects frankly and worthily—a community, in short, where the great aim of all classes and orders with power is by dint of rigorous silence, fast shutting of the eyes, and stern stopping of the ears, somehow to keep the social pyramid on its apex, with the fatal result of preserving for England its glorious fame as a paradise for the well-to-do, a purgatory for the able, and a hell for the poor.[29]

After 1874, the influence of the *Fortnightly* on English politics began to diminish as the result of a phenomenon which seems characteristic of the latter phases of liberal movements generally: the tendency to solidify into dogmatic and doctrinaire positions which lack constructive practical application.[30] As Lionel Trilling has explained the phenomenon, the liberal as a man of principle always runs the risk of being unable to contain the contradictions of life within the logically consistent structure of his principles. He then may unconsciously select the facts to fit his chosen principles. At this point, he loses his usefulness to society because the facts have outrun his dogma.[31]

During the life of the *Fortnightly*, however, the idea of progress challenged the Victorian imagination. From the Victorian man in the street who was awed by the technological progress represented at the great Exhibition at the Crystal Palace in 1851, to the liberal intellectual who pictured society in evolution toward a future perfection through being purged of all its ills by rationalist liberal physicians, mid-Victorians were disposed to worship at the shrine of progress. It was to be some time before Englishmen discovered that the industrial revolution had brought mixed blessings.

In 1877, the idea of progress was critiqued in the pages of the *Fortnightly* itself. Mark Pattison (1813–1884), Anglican clergyman and man of letters, noted that, while the nineteenth century exhibited impressive material progress, economic class distinctions had heightened since the preceding century: "The uniformly diffused well-being of the community in the first half of the eighteenth century compares advantageously with the contrasts of overgrown riches and degraded pauperism which constitute our society." He also questioned if a moral advance were to be discerned; he finally decided that the abolition of the slave trade and slavery in the United States represented moral progress.[32]

The concept of progress had first begun to have important consequences in the eighteenth century. Tyranny in France had led French rationalists to consider radical rearrangements of the political structure in the name of human progress, and this consideration ultimately led to the French Revolution. In England, with a relatively more benevolent government, the idea of progress was given less encouragement by circumstances. The English also saw the role of government in a different light. From Locke's time on, the function of government had been thought of as a limited one in contrast to the French theorists who considered government as a shaper of society.

Despite these differences, the idea of progress emerged to some extent in English thought during the eighteenth century. Adam Smith, for instance, pictured human history as economically progressive in his *Wealth of Nations* (1776)[33]; the idea of progress was expressed as perfectibility in William Godwin's *Political Justice* (1793) and in Shelley's poetry; and the idea of progress later pervaded the whole English Utilitarian movement. When Darwin's evolutionary hypothesis emerged, it seemed to represent to many a valid, scientific basis from which to infer social progress. To the Social Darwinist who emerged, history was progressive and evolutionary. As Stephen stated in his "An Attempted Philosophy of History," the idea of evolution allows the distinction between "the profounder processes, which constitute the organic growth of a society, and those relatively superficial changes which may vary between different states, or in accordance with individual influences or special legislative arrangements, without implying any organic change." [34]

As Stephen began to contribute to the *Fortnightly*, a massive rationalist assault upon religion had commenced in England. The opening shot of the battle was fired in 1869 when John Morley published T. H. Huxley's "On the Physical Basis of Life" in the *Fortnightly*.[35] During the next decade, Charles Algernon Swinburne's *Songs Before Sunrise* (1871), James Thomson's *The City of Dreadful Night* (1875), John Stuart Mill's *Essays on Religion* (1874), Stephen's *Freethinking and Plainspeaking* (1873), as well as his *Fortnightly* essays including the lead essay of *An Agnostic's Apology* (1890) which had first appeared in 1876, were among the works attacking theology. The most active writers leading the attack were Stephen and Huxley, whose work is motivated by an evangelical zeal as they argue in the holy cause of truth. They had been commissioned by science to bring England out of the dark days of theology. These were their feelings, but the surface of their writing is placid as they calmly marshal their arguments.

Huxley's message in his essay was a simple one: life and matter are not separate; matter is the basis of life in all its diversity. As shocking as the implications of Huxley's concept were to Victorian readers, the style itself was not offensive to them; moreover, they expected instruction from their writers and especially the useful knowledge which scientists had to offer. His style is that of the popularizer of science, for his scientific terminology is enlivened by constant references to the average reader as well as by illustrations from literature. His tone is that of the Victorian discourse which plays down controversy by stressing the common ground between the reader and the writer and by minimizing differences as long as possible. Despite these tactics, his whole argument could easily be ignored by the nineteenth-century reader who was likely to object to his materialism. In anticipation of this reaction, he admitted that he had used the language of materialism; but he denied that he was, as a consequence, a materialist. He was instead following the empirical method of David Hume after whom any metaphysical system including materialism was untenable.

Both Stephen and Huxley made strong denials of materialism, and in a strict metaphysical sense they were correct in so doing. Neither wanted to describe the universe as composed of nothing but matter and force.[36] With their rationalistic expectation of the progressive improvement of mankind's lot as society evolved, they could not accept the determinism often associated with the world view known as materialism. They required sea room for man's reason to maneuver the vessel of society safely through the rocks and shoals of the Victorian dilemma. After the advent of Darwin, society had for various thinkers emerged as a potentially dangerous factor of environment. Since man's only recourse was to use his reason to control society so that man might survive, the repugnance of Victorian rationalists for a deterministic world view is comprehensible.

But Huxley and Stephen practiced as materialists: they insisted upon the empirical method which, as they applied it, limited man's knowledge to material phenomena which the senses perceived in the physical world around him. They were not materialists—but only because they refused to proceed to outline the world view which emerges by following their own rules for gathering knowledge. The logical consistency which they demanded of their antagonists would have produced a mechanistic universe from their mode of cognition, and this universe would have denied them not only the use of their reason but also certain feelings. Inclined to view emotions as "gush" or sentimentality, Stephen nonetheless generally reserved for himself the exercise of the moral instinct.

Whatever the merits of Stephen's reasoning, the ultimate fact which emerged for him was his agnosticism. The distinction between agnosticism and atheism is debatable in Stephen's case. As a rationalist, he saw only illogical arguments being used to support religion; as an empiricist, he consulted the data of science and found the basis for a natural rather than a supernatural order in the universe. Instead of saying "I cannot know," he said "I cannot know and neither can you." Furthermore, there is nothing to know beyond the evidences of the senses. What begins as honest doubt quickly becomes dogmatic conviction. Empiricism which should as a method inhibit the human tendency to absolutism somehow fails to do its work for Stephen. But, as William James pointed out in *The Will To Believe* (1897), Stephen was typical of the Victorian agnostic in his absolutism: more concerned to avoid error than to seek truth, Stephen tended generally to limit his cognitions to the kind of data which could be manipulated by the rationalist mind with its love of order; and he then dogmatized about the results.

William James himself enlarged the province of the empiricist to include all experience, including psychological experience. James's definition of pragmatism indicates the way in which he and others sought to enlarge nineteenth-century empiricism:

A pragmatist turns his back resolutely and once for all upon a lot of inveterate habits dear to professional philosophers. He turns away from abstraction and insufficiency, from verbal solutions, from bad *a priori* reasons, from fixed principles, closed systems, and pretended absolutes and origins. He turns towards concreteness and adequacy, towards facts, towards action and towards power. That means the empiricist temper regnant and the rationalist temper sincerely given up. It means the open air and possibilities of nature, as against dogma, artificiality, and the pretense of finality in truth.[37]

In contrast, Stephen's agnosticism was infused with something of the certainty and self-satisfaction of nineteenth-century science which, at least in its pre-Einstein physics, contemplated with pleasure its tidy view of the physical world. This scientific certainty directed his Evangelical sense of the need to enlighten other men. An agnostic in theory, he practiced as an atheist both in his attacks on the institution and on the personal experience of religion. In matters as important as belief or nonbelief, perhaps the most honest service to those who come after is to refrain from dogmatizing. It lessens the risk of becoming a bigot as one attacks bigotry.

The sense of mystery felt by the twentieth-century's most important physicist as he contemplated the physical universe would have been difficult for Stephen to understand. Albert Einstein's own account of his world reflects nothing of the absolutist certainty of the Victorian scientist or his popularizers:

The most beautiful thing we can experience is the mysterious. It is the source of all true art and science. He to whom this emotion is a stranger, who can no longer pause to wonder and stand rapt in awe, is as good as dead: his eyes are closed. This insight into the mystery of life, coupled though it be with fear, has also given rise to religion. To know that what is impenetrable to us really exists, manifesting itself as the highest wisdom and the most radiant beauty which our dull faculties can comprehend only in their most primitive forms—this knowledge, this feeling, is at the center of true religiousness. In this sense, and in this sense only, I belong in the ranks of devoutly religious men.[38]

The Victorian debate between rationalists and believers was not confined to the magazines. Organization of the Metaphysical Society in 1869 provided an opportunity for the leading theologians, philosophers, scientists, rationalist-liberal intellectuals, and men of letters to debate matters of belief in a manner which is most likely improbable today. The sixty-two distinguished Victorians of the group included James Martineau (1805–1900), Unitarian theologian and philosopher; Charles Pritchard (1808–93), astronomer and preacher; Thomas Huxley, physiologist and biologist; W. G. Ward (1812–82), Catholic theologian once active in the Oxford Movement; J. A. Froude, historian; John Tyndall (1820–93), physicist; W. E. Gladstone, liberal statesman; W. K. Clifford (1845–79), mathematician and close friend of Stephen; Frederic Harrison; Tennyson; Ruskin; Stephen's brother Fitzjames; and Leslie himself. The significant omissions include Matthew Arnold, Carlyle, Browning, Newman, Mill, and Spencer.

The essence of the argument upon which the society centered its papers and discussions was: "What is a man entitled to believe about religion, the physical universe, and human nature?" By 1880, the society, unable to agree on fundamentals, dissolved. Alan Brown, who has written the principal account of the organization, asserts that many of the influential minds of the group began as absolutists but acquired respect for compromise in the society's proceedings.[39] Perhaps in practical matters they did so. We see, however, nothing of this compromise among either the believers or the unbelievers in matters of belief.

It was during a meeting of the society that Huxley launched the word "agnostic" to describe his position. As he later explained it, the agnostic followed "not a creed but a method. . . . Positively the principle may be expressed: In matters of the intellect follow your reason as far as it will take you, without any regard to any other consideration. And negatively: In matters of the intellect do not pretend that conclusions are certain which are not demonstrated or demonstrable." [40] In this definition Huxley had modified the meaning he originally intended by the word "agnostic." At first, he had thought of the term to describe a state of mind free from any dogma or conclusions, the reverse of a "gnosis" or intuition of belief. As he pursued science, he found his own belief—not in a world of force and matter such as the German materialists pictured, but in a faith that the physical sciences could ultimately resolve all of man's meaningful questions.

Probably because of his scientific work in biology, Huxley was more truly an empiricist than Stephen. As one of Stephen's biographers points out, Huxley's agnosticism was a method of arguing against specific theological positions; Stephen's agnosticism was a more fully sketched-out system which found theology unreal.[41] His rationalistic tendency to system monger, despite his hatred for metaphysics, led Stephen to commit himself to a complete and final rejection of religion. Huxley's empiricism allows him to sustain the tension of doubt more successfully than Stephen, whatever his faith of the moment. As a recent biographer of Huxley shows us, Huxley was really open to future evidence about religious questions when other agnostics had moved from doubt to denial.[42]

Stephen himself did not join the Metaphysical Society until 1877 and contributed only two papers. His lack of participation in the society may be accounted for because he was contemptuous of discussions which reminded him of undergraduate philosophic debates and because he also had ample opportunity to define and publicize his agnosticism rather fully in *Fraser's* and the *Fortnightly*, in those essays collected as *Freethinking and Plainspeaking*, and in *An Agnostic's Apology*. As Stephen defined agnosticism in the last-mentioned work, it is clear that, despite the Victorian agnostic's intention to go only where his empirical data took him, his feelings allowed him no stop short of another absolutism: religion has no validity as a subject. As he said, an agnostic is "one who asserts—what no one denies—that there are limits to the sphere of human intelligence. He asserts, further, what many theologians have expressly maintained, that those limits are such to include at least what Lewes called 'metempirical' knowledge [metaphysical?]. But he goes further, and asserts, in opposition to theologians, that theology lies within this forbidden sphere." [43]

An Agnostic's Apology [44] presents what for Stephen was the most cogent objection to religion: its inability to deal with the problem of evil. Both natural and human evil in a world created by a just Creator had plagued men since the days of Job. Many writers in the nineteenth century—in England, James Mill (1773–1836), Matthew Arnold, and Thomas Hardy; across the Atlantic, Herman Melville, Nathaniel Hawthorne, Mark Twain, and Henry Adams —responded powerfully to this ancient dilemma. How can a sensitive person reconcile the existence of an all-powerful and all-knowing Creator with the evident fact of pain and suffering in the world? The beneficent natural world of the great chain of being [45] was giving place to a world revealed by science to be governed by natural laws which had no relation to man's values.

The anguish of this discovery emerged in Tennyson's reaction to a pre-Darwinian view of evolution in *In Memoriam* (1850). He asked if man, "Who trusted God was love indeed/And love Creation's final law—/Tho' Nature, red in tooth and claw/With ravine, shriek'd against his creed—," was finally to face extinction himself (LVI, 11. 13–20). Many nineteenth-century rationalists resolved the problem to their satisfaction by denying the existence of an intelligent Creator. We note, for instance, in the *Autobiography* of Charles Darwin that such an argument had force for him, despite the fact that suffering squared with the process of natural selection as he saw it.

The effect of temperament on such an argument is evident, however, in Darwin's thought. Writing between 1876 and 1882,

Darwin, when he asked himself whether life presented the dominant quality of pleasure or pain, concluded that pleasure was foremost.[46] Not so for Stephen. Pain and suffering were the rule for man, as he saw it; and their existence could only be accounted for, from his point of view, by an immoral universe. Under these conditions he could not worship its Creator. Instead, he put his faith in human reason, an idol which is in the twentieth century somewhat tarnished as a consequence of man's demonstration of his capacity for evil on a scale far beyond the Victorian's experience or imagination.

When compared with the earlier *Freethinking and Plainspeaking*, the *Apology* is somewhat less brash in tone. Stephen had moved closer in the later work to the Victorian language of compromise when he said that he hoped to "help clear the air from effete superstitions, to extricate moral truths from the misleading associations with which they have been entangled, and to encourage, as far as in him lies, the spread of truths which may find embodiment in any fresh developments of thought." The image of himself which he hoped to present to his reader in the *Apology* was that of a man of good sense with "a sound estimate" of his own views and qualifications to advance them, of one who makes "a judicious application of his talents to honourable ends." Such a man would be likely to win the approval of other sensible men when he offered them "a vigorous exposition—not given in an irritating and insulting spirit—of the truths which must be the groundwork of a satisfactory religion." While Stephen would count it presumptuous to specify the nature of his religion of the future, it is safe to say that it would contain no supernatural ingredients.[47]

Stephen's position as an agnostic was that he lacked the requisite empirical data to establish an atheist's claim, but it proves to be his dogma in practice. When crucial questions such as religious belief are opened for discussion, objectivity has always been difficult to sustain; at times, in the latter half of our own century, even language itself seems to be dissolving. Surely it is going too far to cite Stephen's *An Agnostic's Apology* as an exhibit of Victorian liberal Christianity. One critic has done this, apparently limiting Christian religious experience to Christianity's ethical content.[48] Stephen would have detested such muddled thinking. His ethical values, wherever he supposed himself to have gotten them, certainly needed, from his point of view, no support from religion. The fact that many of his values were identical to Christian values was apparently a mere historical accident.

While such dogmatism may at first seem unlikely in a rational person, it may have a psychological basis. The theory of the agnostic's position is admirable; in application, it seems to be untenable because of man's apparent necessity to fasten upon some sort of absolutism. Whatever the explanation, Stephen continued rigidly down his path dogmatically asserting the agnostic theory. In a letter to William James in 1898, he insisted that the only opinion that anyone had any right to was no opinion at all; and he was totally oblivious of his own assertion of an opinion.

There seems to be no escape from the conclusion that volition was as decisive in religious questions for Stephen as was discursive reason. For various reasons, he abstained from gathering data on the full range of feelings of the religious sensibility. As Noel G. Annan has observed, Stephen probably was incapable of writing a book like William James's *Varieties of Religious Experience* (1902). The attitude of Stephen and other undergraduates during his Cambridge days toward feelings, which led them to characterize emotions as "gush" and humbug, certainly modified the emotional experience which he permitted himself. At any rate, he was severely handicapped when he addressed himself to the religious experience. Professor Annan's apt evaluation bears repetition: "Ignoring the splendours and glories of religion and the infinite variety of ways in which it corresponds to men's needs, his critique was in this respect poverty-stricken." [49]

Viewed historically, Stephen's attack on the Victorian institution of the church, which regarded itself as the purveyor and arbiter of all truth, clearly has a kind of utility. At a time when religious dogma spoke with authority in English society and operated to inhibit free inquiry, such an attack forced reconsideration of values taken for granted. Such an effect, however, was not to Stephen's purpose; he wanted to replace the existing dogma with his own. From the vantage point of twentieth-century notions of the desirability of a plurality of values, Stephen's position becomes a new tyranny, a new denial of free inquiry. Even in the nineteenth century some saw this—William James, for instance—but Stephen did not. The result is that, where matters of religion are dealt with in his writing, objectivity sometimes suffers.

However limited the Victorian rationalist's world—circum-scribed as it was by a narrow empiricism, a mechanistic psychol-ogy, and a Newtonian physics—may appear to us in the twentieth century; in one sense it was a world larger than its mechanistic implications. Man was still a moral being who was responsible for his actions. The Victorians had not reduced him to an automaton whose every action could be accounted for by environmental con-ditioning or by hereditary factors as many twentieth-century thinkers have since concluded.[50] Environmental explanations of crime had, for example, been advanced by the middle of the century but had not been widely accepted. Middle-class rational-ist intellectuals like Stephen were quite certain of man's moral potential; the realization of this potential, furthermore, was con-tingent only upon the exercise of human reason.

IV *Mountaineer:* The Playground of Europe

Stephen found, as we have observed, his many alpine vacations a refreshing change from his work in London. The pleasure of vigorous climbs and the satisfaction of peaks won, despite fatigue and danger, produced prose which contrasts with the sometimes dessicated and sterile concerns of his rationalistic writings. Some of his earliest work published during his Cambridge days had re-counted his adventures in the Alps, and with the publication of the *Playground of Europe* in 1871, Stephen's love of the mountains had inspired one of the most important books of the century in alpine literature. While he made light of the book to his friends, its appearance certainly gave him timely encouragement during the year when he began active work on *The History of English Thought*.

The events of 1871 suggest the emergence of Stephen from the ranks of journalism as a man of letters. In February, the *Play-ground* appeared; the next month, he assumed the editorship of the *Cornhill Magazine*. This post provided him with a regular sal-ary which gave him a certain independence from the weekly grind of articles. This freedom in turn gave him the necessary time for a vast course of reading among the musty relics of the Deist controversy of the previous century in preparation for the *History of English Thought*. In the *Playground* itself, the discus-sions of the history of men's attitudes toward the Alps also reflect an intensified interest in the history of ideas. Finally, the series

later to be collected as *Hours in a Library* was inaugurated in the
Cornhill in May with an essay about Sir Thomas Browne.

Stephen's *Playground* climaxed the Victorian interest in the
Alps which had begun with travels by scientists seeking evidences
of geologic forces and had evolved into a complex mode of appreciation including elements of esthetic beauty and high adventure.
The *Playground* was one of a series of books which had encouraged more and more Englishmen into the Alps during the 1850's
and 1860's.[51] Peak after unscaled peak fell to adventurous parties,
and the culmination of this first colorful phase of mountaineering
was Edward Whymper's tragic first ascent of the Matterhorn in
1865. The attitude of the Victorian public toward these alpine adventures was mixed, and it was sometimes harshly critical after
the Matterhorn tragedy. For some, like Anthony Trollope, such
adventure gave life zest. For others, like John Ruskin, mountaineering profaned the temples of the Creator. Still others resented
the mountaineer and all the details of his sport.

Stephen's friend John Morley wrote Frederic Harrison in 1872
that Jean-Jacques Rousseau was more genuine in his appreciation
of the mountains than the members of the Alpine Club. As Morley
put it, "there is not one of your pedants of the Alpine Club—from
the sensible and social and civic you, and the cynical, anti-
enthusiastic Stephen—who would not have revelled in giving us a
string of uncouth names, heights, ascents, and only the god of
mountain, cloud, and human pedantry knows what besides. Yet
Rousseau really loved nature, while the Alpine Club takes her as a
pick-me-up after the exhausting imbecilities of the London sea-
son. . . ."[52] If Morley had read the *Playground* by this time, he
had missed an essential ingredient of the book.

Among the earliest of Victorian books which had introduced its
readers to the high Alps was *The Swiss Alps: Travels Through the
Alps of Savoy* (1843) by the Scotch scientist James D. Forbes
(1809–68). His work was the straightforward account of a scientist interested in the natural forces shaping mountain terrain. A
much wider audience was reached by John Ruskin's fourth volume of *Modern Painters* (1856), the book whose influence of Stephen has already been noted. In it, the Victorian reader was given
an opportunity to experience the beauty of the Alps at the same
time that he was edified with the details of alpine data and impressions including plant life, geology, and the appeal of the Alps

to the painter's eye in line, color, and mass. The interest for the reader was heightened by Ruskin's rich poetic prose style.

While some readers among the Victorians, especially members of the Evangelical movement, might have been somewhat ill at ease in the presence of beauty, Ruskin helped them enjoy it in its alpine manifestations by associating it with useful knowledge. Furthermore, for a portion of Ruskin's life the Alps were the source of powerful religious feelings. The conjunction of these feelings with mountain beauty was not without its effect upon many readers. These two books, together with Alfred Wills's *Wanderings Among the High Alps* (1856), paved the way for the Alpine Club's success with its three series of *Peaks, Passes and Glaciers* from 1859 to 1862.

In the year that Stephen's *Playground* appeared, two other mountain works were also published: John Tyndall's *Hours of Exercise* and Edward Whymper's *Scrambles Amongst the Alps.* Tyndall, a scientist of Stephen's acquaintance, enjoyed the Alps principally for the intellectual problems they presented, as well as for the opportunity for physical exercise; but he at times admitted to being powerfully affected by their beauty. Whymper's book revealed even less feeling than Tyndall's, for *Scrambles* is marked by a sparse journalistic style which seldom glances at the beauty of the Alps. Full of the details of mountaineering, it is the work of an adventurer who was determined to make first ascents during the heyday of Victorian mountain climbing. However, the precise nature of the alpine adventure emerged graphically in Whymper's book despite its style. The unique contribution of *Scrambles* to the growing body of mountain lore is to be found in its illustrations: over a hundred woodcuts done by Whymper from sketches he had made on the spot helped the reader to his first really precise visual knowledge of alpine terrain.

Except for Ruskin's book, Stephen's *Playground* represents the work of a much more sophisticated sensibility than its predecessors.[53] In fact, his book is one of the most polished literary products of the intellectual and cultural forces which motivated the Victorian mountaineer. The complexity of Stephen's sensibility as it reacts to the Alps is characteristic of the manner in which many intellectuals of the last half of the century responded to mountain scenery. In the *Playground,* the reader meets humor, pleasure in comradeship, appreciation of the natural forces at work in the mountains, a sense of the beauty of the Alps, and gratitude for the renewing effect of alpine solitude. We should also note that, despite Stephen's rejection of religion, the language which he uses to describe his mountain feelings has religious connotations.

The efforts which Stephen made to avoid unmanly expressions of feeling during his Cambridge days are reflected in the sometimes self-conscious quality of the *Playground*. The writer of this work is easily reconciled with the critic who sympathized with the eighteenth-century disgust for enthusiasm of any sort. When he is faced with a dramatic alpine scene of the sort which would have evoked raptures from the Romantic sensibility of a Byron or a Shelley, he may instead respond with a schoolboy joke. It is as if he meant to bait those who would, like Ruskin, wax ecstatic over the beauty of the Alps.

In the *Playground*, Stephen has set himself the task of explaining the precise nature of the mountaineer's pleasures to the general reader. In his enumeration of the ways in which the mountaineer could enjoy alpine scenery, ways denied to the non-climber, he points out that the mountains present their true proportions only when seen from above: "Creeping about amongst the roots of the hills, you half miss the hills themselves; you quite fail to understand the massiveness of the mountain chains, and, therefore, the wonderful energy of the forces that have heaved the surface of the world into these distorted shapes. And it is to a half-conscious sense of the powers that must have been at work that a great part of the influence of mountain scenery is due." [54] In this passage a characteristic response of the secularized Victorian mountaineer is to be observed: from a new appreciation of the physical proportions and mass of the Alps, he moves to appreciation of the natural forces which have shaped them.

Occasionally, the reactions of Stephen go a step further. Sometimes the mountains represent to him an environment beyond man's capacity to control, an environment which should give man a realistic sense of his own insignificance in the total scheme: "The mountains represent the indomitable force of nature to which we are forced to adapt ourselves; they speak to man of his littleness and his ephemeral existence; they rouse us from the placid content in which we may be lapped when contemplating the fat fields which we have conquered and the rivers which we have forced to run according to our notions of convenience." [55] Such perspective is useful to the intellectual who for the most part is denied it within his study. Probably few of those twentieth-century commentators who confidently predict the imminent control of physical nature have personal experiences such as Stephen's to consult. Most have never, for instance, been close to destruction by the forces of nature. There is a world of insight to be gathered from one's presence at the awesome buildup of electrical potential prior to a thunderstorm on a granite ridge well above timber line. As Stephen observes when discussing the poetry based on Mont Blanc: "It is true, indeed, that Mont Blanc sometimes is too savage for poetry. He can speak in downright tragic earnestness; and anyone who has been caught in a storm on some of his higher icefields, who has trembled at the deadly swoop of the gale, or at the ominous sound which heralds an avalanche, or at the remorseless settling down of the blinding snow, will agree that at times he passes the limits of the terrible which comes fairly within the range of art." [56]

In Stephen's case, the insights into nature which science had presented him were augmented by personal experience, and the result was anything but contempt. Instead, he retains a feeling of awe analogous to the earlier feeling of the sublime, an emotion which men had first felt late in the seventeenth century when regarding the Alps as the work of an all-powerful Creator.[57] Emphasis upon man's smallness amid powerful natural forces is fairly consistent in the *Playground*. His scientific mode of apprehending mountain beauty is evident in this passage:

[Mont Blanc] is a part of the great machinery in which my physical frame is inextricably involved, and not the less interesting because a part which I am unable to subdue to my purposes. The whole universe, from the stars and the planets to the mountains and the insects which creep about their root, is but a network of forces eternally acting and reacting upon each other. The mind of man is a musical instrument upon which all external objects are beating out infinitely complex harmonies and discords. Too often, indeed, it becomes a mere barrel-organ mechanically repeating the tunes which have once been impressed upon it. But in proportion as it is more vigorous or delicate, it should retain its sensibility to all the impulses which may be conveyed to it from the most distant sources. And certainly a healthy organization should not be deaf to those more solemn and melancholy voices which speak through the wildest aspects of nature.[58]

The solitude which he found in the Alps also held great appeal for Stephen. Despite his pleasure in solitude, however, he found alpine beauty to be enhanced by man and his activities:

The snows of Mont Blanc and the cliffs of the Matterhorn would have their charm in the midst of a wilderness; but their beauty is amazingly increased when a weather-stained chalet rises in the foreground; when the sound of cowbells comes down through the thin air; or the little troop of goats returns at sunset to the quiet village. . . . The snowy ranges of California or the more than alpine heights of the Caucasus may doubtless be beautiful, but to my imagination at least they seem to be unpleasantly bare and chill, because they are deprived of all those intricate associations which somehow warm the bleak ranges of Switzerland.[59]

One of Stephen's most powerful emotions in the presence of the Alps is one which closely parallels the solace and rejuvenation of the religious experience. After detailing the typography visible from the summit of the Schreckhorn, he said:

You are in the centre of a whole district of desolation, suggesting a landscape from Greenland, or an imaginary picture of England in the glacial epoch, with shores yet unvisited by the irrepressible Gulf stream. The charm of such views—little as they are generally appreciated by professed admirers of the picturesque—is to my taste unique, though not easily explained to unbelievers. They have a certain soothing influence like slow and stately music, or one of the strange opium dreams described by De Quincey . . . there is something almost unearthly in the sight of enormous spaces of hill and plain, apparently unsubstantial as a mountain mist, glimmering away to the indistinct horizon, and as it were spellbound by an absolute and eternal silence . . . on that perfect day on the top of the Schreckhorn, where not a wreath of vapour was to be seen under the whole vast canopy of the sky, a delicious lazy sense of calm repose was the appropriate frame of mind.[60]

The nature of Stephen's emotional responses to alpine terrain clearly paralleled the religious experience of others. Furthermore, for him it was a faith that needed no justification—unlike his agnosticism. He asserted, for instance, "the love of mountains is ultimately connected with all that is noblest in human nature." His love of the Alps derived further reinforcement when he contrasted their unique beauty with Victorian society which for Stephen was beginning to be pervaded by a sense of conformity. As he put it, "Mountain scenery is the antithesis not so much of the plains as of the commonplace. Its charm lies in its vigorous originality. . . ." [61]

Much Victorian alpine prose is heavily freighted with worn-out adjectives taken from the Romantics, but Stephen's style represents a successful avoidance of this problem. He was able to use adjectives with precision and sensitivity and he also employed active verbs. While his similes and metaphors lack the drama and imagination of Ruskin's, they are nonetheless effective. He made every effort to localize his settings, with the result that he achieved greater concreteness than many of his contemporaries. Although he solved some of the problems of the genre, his style is subject to one fault: it lacks consistency of tone. The reader becomes engrossed in an impressionistic passage which evokes both the alpine setting and the writer's response to it with great power, only to be brought abruptly to earth with Stephen's announcement that he is "verging on the poetical" or has "already been too daring." It seems that he was fearful of falling into a Ruskinian rhetoric. During a discussion of the problem of style in mountain writing,[62] he expressed admiration for the eloquence of Ruskin but felt that few were capable of it. Most English writers, on the contrary, affect a cynical manner in their mountain descriptions and attempt to entertain their readers, hoping thus to avoid becoming ridiculous through failing to evoke the sublime. When Stephen said that those who joked were nonetheless sensitive to mountain beauty, he is supported by his own writing. It is clear that he possessed great sensitivity, and consistent expression of it is the only problem in his work.

For a person described by one of his biographers as one who enjoyed the Alps only as an athlete, Stephen's prose reveals precision and sensitivity. For example, we have the following description of alpine foregrounds:

Resting in sublime indolence you may admire the beauty of Alpine foregrounds. . . . Every ledge is enamelled by some harmonious lichen. The miniature caves are spread with soft beds of moss, and delicate ferns look out from unexpected crannies. Brilliant flowers (the names of every one of which are entirely unknown to me), supply points of glowing colour along the ridges and salient angles, and some graceful tree manages to find sufficient nourishment for its roots, and rises like the crest of a helmet above the crag.[63]

Whatever Stephen's feelings about Ruskin's style, it did not seem to trouble him to borrow one of Ruskin's repeatedly used similes for this passage: the crest of a helmet. Stephen's imagination could also sustain an evocative impressionism such as in the following description of the Alps in winter:

The very daylight has an unreal glow. The noisy summer life is suspended. A scarce audible hush seems to be whispered throughout the region. The first glacier stream that you meet strikes the keynote of the prevailing melody. In summer the torrent comes down like a charge of cavalry—all rush and roar and foam and fury—turbid with the dust ground from the mountain's flanks by the ice-share, and spluttering and writhing in its bed like a creature in the agonies of strangulation. In winter it is transformed into the likeness of one of the gentle brooks that creeps around the roots of Scawfell, or even one of those sparkling trout streams that slide through a water-meadow beneath Stonehenge. It is perfectly transparent. It babbles round rocks instead of clearing them at a bound. . . . The pulse of the mountains is beating low. . . . This dreamlike impression is everywhere pervading and dominant. It is in proportion to the contrary impression of stupendous, if latent, energy which the Alps make upon one in summer.[64]

The power of his alpine prose is most evident in his own favorite passage in the *Playground*—the description of a sunset on Mont Blanc:

The long series of western ranges melted into a uniform hue as the sun declined in their rear. Amidst their folds the Lake of Geneva became suddenly lighted up in a faint yellow gleam. To the east a blue gauze seemed to cover valley by valley as they sank into night and the intervening ridges rose with increasing distinctness, or rather it seemed that some fluid of exquisite delicacy of colour and substance was flooding all the lower country beneath the great mountains. Peak by peak the high snowfields caught the rosy glow and shone like signal-fires across the dim breadths of delicate twilight. Like Xerxes, we looked over the countless host sinking into rest, but with the rather different thought, that a hundred years hence they would probably be doing much the

same thing, whilst we should long have ceased to take any interest in
the performance. And suddenly began a more startling phenomenon.
A vast cone, with its apex pointing away from us, seemed to be suddenly
cut out from the world beneath; night was within its borders and the
twilight still all around; the blue mists were quenched where it fell,
and for the instant we could scarcely tell what was the origin of this
strange appearance. . . . Of course a moment's reflection explained
the meaning of this uncanny intruder; it was the giant shadow of Mont
Blanc, testifying to his supremacy over all meaner eminences.[65]

Aside from the intrinsic worth of Stephen's *Playground* as a
sensitive account of pioneer alpine exploration, the book is also of
importance in the development of Stephen as a historian of ideas.
Nineteenth-century writers from Wordsworth on had noticed an
important shift of taste associated with the emergence of Roman-
ticism. Travelers in the seventeenth century had found the Alps
repugnant esthetically; but, in the next century, such scenes began
to appeal to men's imaginations.

The new taste was first noticed by Wordsworth in 1844, but the
poet offered no explanation.[66] A little later John Ruskin, in his
Modern Painters III (1856), dealt with the question as it was
reflected in painting. He found that, from the Classical through
the medieval periods, painters tended to relegate mountains to
insignificance in their backgrounds. Then, in nineteenth-century
painting, artists began to move mountains into their foregrounds.
Ruskin attributed this state of affairs to the contemporary interest
in the physical world which had been generated by science. As he
said, man "used to take no interest in anything but what immediately concerned himself. *Now*, he has deep interest in the abstract
natures of things, inquires as eagerly into the laws which regulate
the economy of the material world, as into those of his own being,
and manifests a passionate admiration of inanimate objects,
closely resembling, in its elevation and tenderness, the affection
which he bears to those living souls with which he is brought into
the nearest fellowship." [67]

Ruskin's explanation partially accounts for the nineteenth-
century phenomenon, but it does not explain the eighteenth-
century enthusiasm for mountain beauty. Various literary historians in the latter part of the Victorian period suggested a theory
which explained the new taste in English letters as the influence
of a single pioneer; and the several candidates included Thomas

Gray, James Thomson, and Rousseau. Stephen himself nominated Rousseau as the chief literary influence in the first chapter of the *Playground,* but his view was generally more sophisticated than most. In a comparison of mountain attitudes held by the seventeenth-century theologian, Thomas Burnet (c. 1635–1715); the Romantic novelist, Sir Walter Scott; and the Victorian observer, Stephen was fully conscious of the fact that the appeal of the Alps was based on more than just a closer acquaintance as suggested by Ruskin.

Stephen recognized that both religious and scientific concepts had played their part in the shift of taste. Alluding to Burnet's *Sacred Theory of the Earth* (1684), he said: "Think of the mountains as, in sober earnestness, ruins of the antediluvian world, and they are really terrible. When they have declined into the romantic stage the same expression is merely a lively image of their apparent chaos. At a later period they gain an interest of a different order, when the mounds are indicative of ancient glacial forces and every rock speaks to the observer of the slow lapse of geological periods." [68]

From the vantage point of the twentieth century, Stephen's analysis is deficient in only one respect: subsequent scholarship has demonstrated the importance of the idea of the sublime, a religious feeling expressed in English literature through admiration for the mighty features of landscape such as the Alps. Stephen observed the terror which Burnet felt as he viewed the Alps, but he did not identify this emotion with the sublime, later an important literary convention. It must be granted that a clear understanding of the importance of this esthetic concept was not to emerge for many years. In 1959, Marjorie Nicolson's *Mountain Gloom and Mountain Glory* distinguished between the concept of the sublime inherited by Englishmen from Longinus, primarily a matter of rhetoric, and a native tradition of the sublime which antedates the Classical usage. She conclusively demonstrated the seventeenth-century English transfer of the religious feeling of awe from man's Maker to the new heavens revealed by astronomy and then the association of these same feelings with mighty terrestrial objects such as the Alps. In view of the scholarship devoted to the topic between Stephen's day and the present, his insights into this esthetic problem clearly suggest his emerging talent as a historian of ideas.

CHAPTER 3

Victorian Rationalist Historian of Ideas

THE events of 1871, including the publication of the *Playground*, mark the passage in Stephen's career from journalist to intellectual historian and man of letters. These two interests which we have watched emerge were to hold Stephen's attention for the balance of his life. In this fifth year of his marriage and in the seventh of his London residence, he began his best-known work, *The History of English Thought in the Eighteenth Century*. An ambitious project, it was not to be completed for five years, for the extended account of the Deist controversy of the previous century demanded a heavy course of reading in the musty theological literature of the period. Upon receipt of the work, one of his American friends, Lowell, wrote him: "How the deuce you read all those books and escaped to tell us of 'em is a conundrum I shall carry unsolved to my grave." [1] The project was also undertaken at a time when Stephen's writing for the periodicals had accelerated to a furious pace. His articles and reviews appeared in the *Alpine Journal*, the *Cornhill*, the *Fortnightly*, *Fraser's*, and *Macmillan's* that year. The appointment as editor of the *Cornhill* with its £500 salary gave timely relief from the pressure of his journalism and thus enabled him to pursue the more scholarly project.

In no sense of the phrase is Stephen to be regarded, however, as a time-server in his capacity as editor of the *Cornhill*. The quality of his services to a publication which permitted no expression of his own most serious interests as a writer is characteristic of his sense of duty. Under his command, the magazine established the literary standard among the Victorian family magazines. As editor, he also had the opportunity to further some important Victorian literary careers, including an acquaintance of his American visits, Henry James; the literary careers of Thomas Hardy, Robert Louis Stevenson, and W. E. Henley were also given decisive encouragement from their appearances in the *Cornhill*.

During these crucial years, the pattern of Stephen's friendships continued to exhibit a reserve which he put aside only for a few of similar interests such as Norton and Morley. At this time, the larger circle of his friends included Harrison, Meredith, and his other American correspondents, Holmes and Lowell. The Americans made occasional visits to London, and their letters gave him much encouragement in his literary projects, especially those of Lowell and Norton. Outside this intellectual companionship, his response to the London social scene which his connections had opened for him suggests that he was becoming, if anything, more introverted. A few years later he was to describe London society in these terms:

London has become a chaos; society means intercourse for a couple of hours with a fortuitous concurrence of human atoms; little circles are swept away in the great current; you make a small journey to a friend's house; you are set down by a stranger and have to beat the bush for an hour before you discover what little segment of the vast circle of human interests is common to both. You must be on your guard in view of possible collisions, and keep to the superficial which hurt no sensibilities because they excite no real interest.[2]

One of the most consequential intellectual relationships at this time, considering the many biographies to be written by Stephen in the years ahead, was that which existed with Thomas Carlyle. Stephen was the disciple of Mill, but he saw much more of his philosophical antagonist, Carlyle, at his Cheyne Row house. The old prophet fascinated Stephen. While the young man found it necessary to conceal his own views to avoid conversational explosions, he was nonetheless drawn to Cheyne Row by Carlyle's personal force, by his sense of humor, and by his ability to evoke memorable biographical portraits.

In 1871, when Stephen defended Carlyle in a letter to Lowell, who had just criticized Carlyle, Stephen admitted his own distaste for the prophet's political views but said, "I can't help loving the old fellow; and amongst the other reasons for this is that of all us literary professionals in London he is in his life the manliest and simplest. It is a pleasure to see anybody who has the courage to live so little spoilt by the flattery which might have choked him and made him into a windbag" (Maitland, 228).

The visits to Cheyne Row became more and more difficult. In

1873, Stephen wrote Norton that he had not given Carlyle a copy of his *Freethinking and Plainspeaking* out of a desire to avoid further unpleasantness. A rift had developed between the two which Stephen regretted. Despite "a really strong affection" for Carlyle, the younger man was ill at ease at being lectured to; he withdrew into himself in their meetings; and he became, as he said, "dogged and speechless." He felt that Carlyle disliked him; consequently, his irregular visits became a less and less pleasant duty. Two years later their relations became yet more strained as a result of Stephen's attempt to introduce Robert Louis Stevenson to his distinguished countryman, for Carlyle resented being put on display. Nonetheless, when Carlyle died a few years later, Stephen regretted his death more than that of George Eliot; and he was sorry that his visits to Cheyne Row had ceased.

I *Editor of the* Cornhill

The founding of the *Cornhill* had been one of the major literary events of 1860. Its success as a family magazine was based on the popularity of its editor, the novelist William Makepeace Thackeray, a new low price of one shilling for a general magazine, as well as the Victorian public's enthusiasm for the serial novel. Furthermore, the *Cornhill's* generous rates of pay attracted the best-known literary figures of the day. The first issue, for example, included opening installments of two novels, Thackeray's *Lovel the Widower* and Trollope's *Framley Parsonage.* Other famous contributors to appear included Tennyson, Matthew Arnold, John Ruskin, and George Eliot. George Smith, the publisher, was not disappointed with his scheme; for the circulation of the magazine exceeded one hundred thousand for several years.

When Stephen took charge of the *Cornhill* eleven years later, however, competition from magazines of similar format such as *Temple Bar, Argosy, Macmillan's Magazine,* and the *Fortnightly,* whose reader appeal ranged from light to serious, had made heavy inroads on the *Cornhill's* audience; its circulation was down to about twenty-five thousand. Paradoxically under Stephen's command, when its literary quality led the field of family magazines, the circulation dropped still more; for when he left in 1882, it was twelve thousand. In general, Stephen's editorial judgments were seemingly not in tune with the changes in public taste. In the 1880's both the literary essay and the serial novel lost favor with the readers of the *Cornhill*, yet both continued to form the staple fare of the magazine.[3]

To Stephen's credit, his sojourn with the *Cornhill* was responsible for a substantial number of high-quality literary essays being brought before the Victorian reader. The first issue under his direction (March, 1871) helped to set the character of the magazine for many years. It included a three-part essay on Nathaniel Hawthorne by J. T. Fields. Among the regular contributors was John Addington Symonds (1840–93), who had begun his essays on Italy and art under Thackeray. Stephen's own "Hours in a Library" series commenced in May of that year. The essays of Robert Louis Stevenson and Edmund Gosse (1849–1928) began to appear in 1874. The result was that five important collections of essays were ultimately collected from the *Cornhill* articles of the four writers.[4] In addition to these essays which establish the distinctive tone of the *Cornhill* under Stephen, the magazine continued its prior makeup with serial novels, short novels, and a variety of articles on noncontroversial subjects. These included a number of travel pieces set in exotic parts of the globe.

Modern criticism of Stephen's editorial work on the *Cornhill* usually calls attention to his compromises in taste and to his censorship, which was most active where religion or moral questions were involved. Both of these topics are fraught with subjective possibilities in any age. But special difficulties are found when we deal with a period so close to our own and with one which is still being rehabilitated after years of disrepute. And however enlightened twentieth-century men may fancy themselves, they have yet to deal wisely with the problem of taste which bedeviled the Victorians.

The most serious charges brought against Stephen's editorship have been directed toward his censorship. Here again the context is important. Under Thackeray, a very cautious editorial policy was followed which avoided any sort of controversial subject matter for the sake of the magazine's family audience. Thus Thackeray rejected a poem of Mrs. Browning's, and he terminated an essay series of Ruskin's (*Unto This Last*) because of protests from his readers. Stephen was fully aware of this before he took the post; for at his appointment, he said: "What can one make of a magazine which excludes the only subjects in which reasonable men take any interest: politics and religion?" (Maitland, 257–58).

Censorship under Stephen began his first year with the *Cornhill*. Matthew Arnold had often appeared in the magazine with his literary essays, his criticism of English society and politics in the essays later published as *Culture and Anarchy* (1869), and his controversial *St. Paul and Protestantism* (1870) in which he attacked the institution of Christianity for the way in which its dogmas distorted the essence of Christ's teachings. Stephen published the first two installments of *Literature and Dogma* in 1871, but a promised third installment never materialized.

Recalling his editing experiences over thirty years later, Stephen said: "Matthew Arnold had to part company after a time, to my regret, because he wished to discourse upon topics to which we had to give a wide berth." [5] In this case, Stephen seems to have been even more conservative than his predecessors. But, as Oscar Maurer has noted, the avoidance of religious controversy was the result both of his sense of obligation to the *Cornhill's* publisher, George Smith, and of his honest acceptance of the *Cornhill's* editorial policies.[6] When we remember that Stephen was publishing a good deal of rationalist criticism of English theology in *Fraser's* and in the *Fortnightly*, it seems that we would have to be something of a fire-eating liberal to accuse Stephen of intellectual cowardice on the basis of his reluctance to allow theological controversy in the *Cornhill*. Furthermore, the financial security of the appointment made possible his most important scholarly work.

Stephen's failure to attack religion in the *Cornhill* is dereliction enough for some modern critics, but for those who follow the Freudian dispensation, his gravest sin is reticence in sexual matters. One of his biographers observes that Stephen's intolerance of French novels, particularly what he considered their unhealthy sensuality, makes it clear that Stephen's editorial judgment had a personal basis and was not the result of surrendering to public taste. Instead, it followed from his own inhibitions.[7] Professor Maurer points out what is abundantly clear from Stephen's comments on the relation between art and morality: that Stephen's concern with morality in art had a much wider base—the larger social context. He always asked himself if a particular work of art advanced or retarded the general happiness of society. Finally, as Maurer stresses, it was with Stephen a matter of avoiding certain words—"verbal shock"—not moral situations themselves.[8] Again we see the Victorian language of compromise in action. In a century which is beginning to insist upon all the four-letter words of our Anglo-Saxon heritage, the Victorian approach probably seems craven. Perhaps, however, the Victorian sensibility was more subtle in that it did not need all the details made graphic.

To his credit, Stephen gave editorial encouragement to the literary careers of Thomas Hardy, Henry James, Robert Louis Stevenson, and W. E. Henley. At their first meeting in 1873, Hardy discovered an aspect of Stephen's character which their correspondence had not revealed—he found that he had to deal with an editor who was a "character": "He welcomed me with one hand, holding back the barking 'Troy' with the other. The dog's name I, of course, had never heard till then, and I said, 'That is the name of my wicked soldier-hero.' He answered caustically: 'I don't think my Troy will feel hurt at the coincidence, if yours doesn't.' I rejoined, 'There is also another coincidence. Another Leslie Stephen lives near here, I find.' 'Yes,' he said, 'he's the spurious one'" (Maitland, 273). The meeting led Hardy to feel an affection for Stephen which he had not anticipated from his business dealings with the editor of the *Cornhill*.

With three novels almost behind him, Hardy was still relatively unknown when Stephen first had written him the year before praising his *Under the Greenwood Tree* and asked if he had another serial under way. The *Cornhill* appearance of *Far from the Madding Crowd* in 1874, which finally resulted from Stephen's request, was decisive in Hardy's career; for the popularity of this novel was his first real success.[9] The next novel, *The Hand of Ethelberta*, which appeared the following year did not fare so well with the *Cornhill* audience. Then in 1877 when the opening chapters of *The Return of the Native* were offered by Hardy, Stephen refused it as potentially dangerous. Although they could not agree on some literary matters, the impact of Stephen's rationalism on Hardy was the greatest of any of his contemporaries.[10]

Stephen's letters to Hardy both indicate the nature of their literary differences and illustrate Stephen's editorial practices. His concern with "verbal shock" is especially evident on these particular passages that reply to Hardy's expression of resentment at what he considered Stephen's prudish restraint in sexual matters during the publication of *Far from the Madding Crowd:*

I have ventured to leave out a line or two in the last batch of proofs, from an excessive prudery of which I am ashamed; but one is forced to be absurdly particular. May I suggest that Troy's seduction of the young woman will require to be treated in a gingerly fashion when, as I suppose must be the case, he comes to be exposed to his wife? I mean that the thing must be stated, but that the words must be careful. Excuse this wretched shred of concession to popular stupidity; but I am a slave. (Maitland, 273–74)

Later, when the novel that was amended to suit Hardy appeared in book form, the *Times* reviewed this passage favorably. Hardy's pleasure was blunted by Stephen's reply: "I spoke as an editor, not as a man. You have no more consciousness of these things than a child" (Maitland, 274). These and other passages in Stephen's correspondence indicate that his censorship of Hardy's work was strongly motivated by the reaction of the *Cornhill's* public which he had initially agreed to please.

The career of the novelist Henry James was also given material assistance by Stephen. The two had first met in Boston during Stephen's second American visit in 1868. Their acquaintance was renewed in 1876 when James moved to London. At this time James's literary reputation was based primarily on his American periodical publication in the *Atlantic Monthly* and the *Nation.* His English reputation commenced with the serial appearance of *Daisy Miller* (1878) in the *Cornhill.* As has often happened with Americans, the story had first been refused by *Lippincott's Magazine* in Philadelphia.[11] *Washington Square* was another important work which made its first appearance in the *Cornhill* (1880).

Two other figures of consequence who began their careers in the pages of the *Cornhill* were Robert Louis Stevenson and W. E. Henley. Because both were handicapped by poverty and ill health, Stephen's backing was especially meaningful; and their success provided him with one of his greatest satisfactions as editor of the *Cornhill.* From Stevenson's first appearance in the magazine until the conclusion of Stephen's editorship in 1882, twenty essays, four stories, and a poem were published. This timely encouragement came before Stevenson achieved his wider reputation in the 1880's with *Treasure Island* (1883) and *Dr. Jekyll and Mr. Hyde* (1886).

In January, 1875, Stephen, while in Edinburgh lecturing on the Alps, took Stevenson to the Infirmary to visit another contributor from whom he had accepted a poem for the *Cornhill*, W. E. Henley. Stephen, hoping to provide Henley with intellectual companionship, instigated between the two what Henley's biographer, John Connell, calls "a romantic friendship, in the strict sense of that term." The success of Henley's poem, "Hospital Outlines: Sketches and Portraits," established him as a poet.[12] The blunt realism of this poem, the publication of which Stephen's first biographer regarded as his most daring editorial decision, suggests the outer limits of his censorship.

Stephen's grossest sins of taste for the modern sensibility can be observed in the dominance of second-rate popular novels such as those produced by his sister-in-law, Mrs. Anne Thackeray Ritchie, and by Mrs. Margaret Oliphant, both of whom had begun writing for the *Cornhill* under previous editors. Mrs. Eliza Lynn Linton and William Black are the best known of the group introduced by Stephen. While the objective fact is that these novelists produced an ephemeral entertainment, it is also true that they were very successful with *Cornhill* readers. And Stephen had at the outset accepted the nature of the *Cornhill* audience, but he was clearly true to his own tastes when he offset these novels with quality literary criticism often directed toward the literature of previous ages. Thus the makeup of the magazine had the rather subtle potential of improving its readers' tastes without being offensive. After these factors are recognized, such genuine errors of taste as remain represent the sort of mistake for which every practicing editor doubtless hopes to be excused.

Stephen has also been criticized for giving in to the plot demands of serial publication. Implicit in such criticism seems to be the feeling that Stephen should have managed to stand aside from his age completely in the direction of a business concern which needed an audience from that age. Moreover, what major Victorian novelist really escaped the structural limitations of serial publication? From Dickens to Hardy, all of the novelists lived with this fact of the Victorian literary world.

In October, 1882, Stephen was chagrined by his discovery of the magazine's decline in circulation. The year before he had begun during a summer vacation to develop the idea of what was to become the *Dictionary of National Biography*. In the summer of 1882 he began to discuss it with George Smith. Then, when the dictionary scheme was again broached in October, Smith mentioned the *Cornhill's* problems. As early as August, Stephen himself had begun to view the dictionary project as an occasion to drop the *Cornhill*. When he learned of its decreasing circulation, he felt that he had no alternative but to resign. The candor of his letter to Smith after their October meeting is characteristic. In it he considered the possibility of converting the *Cornhill* to a more intellectual magazine like the *Fortnightly*. This conversion, he felt, would frighten away the *Cornhill* readership because he as editor would wish to publish articles on politics and theology like those in the *Fortnightly*. He also thought of making it a lighter magazine, but he realized that he was not suited for that task either. His summary: "as our present road leads downhill, and I cannot take either of the ways which might possibly lead upwards, the conclusion is clear." [13] Thus, Stephen resigned the *Cornhill* post and became editor of the mammoth project to be known as the *Dictionary of National Biography*.

During the busy period of his *Cornhill* editorship, his publications had included *Freethinking and Plainspeaking*, the three series of *Hours in a Library*, and the two volumes of *The History of English Thought in the Eighteenth Century*, which had gone into a second edition by 1880. His interest in biography had also intensified. The English Men of Letters series had been conceived by his friend John Morley in 1877. By 1882 Stephen had his *Samuel Johnson, Alexander Pope*, and *Swift* in the series. Finally, his *Science of Ethics* appeared in the same year. As all these publications indicate, the *Cornhill* years had been momentous but sad ones for Stephen personally. He was profoundly depressed by the loss of his first wife, Minny, whose death in 1875 had for a time rendered his life meaningless. In 1878, he married Julia Prinsep Jackson, who herself had been a widow for seven years and who was to be the mother of Virginia Woolf.

II   History of English Thought in the Eighteenth Century

Of all Stephen's works, the *History of English Thought in the Eighteenth Century* probably retains the greatest general interest for twentieth-century readers. It represents an important part of the general salvage job done during the second half of the nineteenth century which recovered eighteenth-century reputations from the depths to which they had sunk after being pushed overboard by the Romantics. To this historical interest should also be added the fact that Stephen's account of the century's intellectual history is substantially acceptable to twentieth-century scholars, requiring relatively minor shifts of emphasis to satisfy most contemporary students of the period. So great a thinker as Alfred North Whitehead (1861–1947), the English philosopher and mathematician, noted that Stephen's work was one of the few books which had influenced his attitude toward history.[14]

From Stephen's Cambridge days, he had wished to tackle a major writing project, but the demands of journalism had interfered. Finally, his feeling for the eighteenth century had stimulated what was to have been an essay on the Deists. As it evolved, his account of the subject grew into two volumes and 925 pages and embraced the theological, philosophical, political, and economic thought of the age. According to one historian, it was planned as a background to a history of nineteenth-century thought.[15] If this were the case, his other writing projects deflected his aim; only *The English Utilitarians* (1900) was written. The scope of *English Thought*, with its reconstruction of the intellectual battles and with its many biographical sketches of the participants, represents what would be considered an audacious writing project by many twentieth-century scholars. Stephen himself later regarded the work as deficient in research, but his tendency to deprecate all of his writing must be recalled to balance the record.

The nature of Stephen's writing which had preceded *English Thought* helps to account for its enduring worth. In formulating and airing his agnosticism before hostile audiences, he had learned to present abstract ideas to the average reader with force and clarity. His rationalism had also focused his attention upon the historical process of the evolution of ideas, and his emerging interest in biography breathed life into a work which could easily have been as stagnant as the issues he recounted. *English Thought*, an apparently objective history of ideas, also functions as a polemic of the Victorian rationalist's general attack on theology. By describing theology as near death in the eighteenth century, Stephen hoped to insure its funeral in the nineteenth century. Because of this hope, it is to Stephen's credit as a writer that *English Thought* has not become a period piece of Victorian rationalism.

Stephen was fortunate to have undertaken his historical project when he did. By mid-century, English historians like Henry Thomas Buckle (1821–62) and W. E. H. Lecky (1838–1903) were beginning to achieve a breadth of vision which distinguished them from the great eighteenth-century historians such as Hume and Gibbon who had regarded history as a sequence of unrelated events. These Victorians began to treat history as the comprehensive account of the operation of the social organism—including its politics, its economics, its artistic activity, and its physical environment. Such a view stimulated the formulation of theories to explain the relationships of the various spheres of human activity as well as their total pattern.

In the works of Buckle, Lecky, and J. S. Mill, Stephen encountered one of these theories: the idea that human reason was the mainspring of progress; in other words, ideas shaped history. More particularly, these middle-class liberals felt that progress could only come when the English mind had slipped its theological shackles. It will be recalled, too, that Comte had pictured society as evolving from theology. Then, with Darwin's theory, which seemed to confirm Comte, Stephen modified his faith in the potency of reason. The reader of *English Thought* is cautioned by Stephen that ideas do not necessarily control events; they are decisive only when other factors of the social milieu are favorable. The course of history was a slow organic evolution of society in the matrix of its environment—from simple to complex ideas and institutions.[16] Precise data about this evolution could only come when historians begin to employ a comparative approach: the "historical method."

Whichever theory one used to explain history's events, the historical method itself had come into its own by the time Stephen wrote *English Thought*. One of the best contemporary statements of the method is to be seen in Mill's essay "Theism" (1874): "The philosophical study of history, one of the most important creations of recent times, has rendered possible an impartial estimate of the doctrines and institutions of the past, from a relative instead of an absolute point of view—as incidents of human development at which it is useless to grumble, and which may deserve admiration and gratitude for their effects in the past, even though they may be thought incapable of rendering similar services in the future." [17]

Stephen's Social Darwinism put him into a quandary when he came to write *English Thought*. First of all, he was compelled by his rationalistic faith to continue his intellectual war on theology in a history of ideas. One article of this faith held that ideas shaped history; but, after the Darwinian dispensation, this article had become unacceptable. The upshot was that, while his preface helps to establish him as one of the English pioneers of the concept that ideas are but the by-product of history and not its prime mover, *English Thought* disappoints its readers by concentrating on the logical development and the logical fallacies of the Deist controversy with but incidental references to causal social conditions.

The first to notice this conflict, Professor John Bicknell, explained this lack as a consequence of Stephen's feeling that the Deist attacks on orthodoxy in the previous century were part of the same war being conducted by himself and other Victorian rationalists. Hence Stephen was compelled to retrace the Deist arguments to compensate for their weaknesses of logic and knowledge. In this way, he could finish the job begun by the Deists. Ideologically committed to this task, he played down his own intellectual awareness of the importance of social conditions in eighteenth-century thought in order to concentrate on the logical fallacies of the Deists and their orthodox adversaries.[18] Professor Bicknell's explanation is clearly valid; but we should note that Stephen—despite his respect for those explanations of literature which tried to take into account the social environment—felt that historical study was not yet sufficiently evolved to permit precision of statement about such matters.[19]

Judgment of the objectivity of Stephen's approach to this facet of intellectual history depends to some extent upon the reader's own taste and beliefs. For example, one twentieth-century reviewer celebrates Stephen as a "God-killer" in a review of a new edition of *English Thought*. He finds Stephen's kind of intellectual history, because of his "personal involvement," superior to that of scholars like A. O. Lovejoy. Clearly, there is merit in commitment like Stephen's; it gives his work life. But to praise Stephen for "tolerance" is surely to ignore the fact of his nearly lifelong attack on theology.[20]

Not surprisingly, students of the eighteenth century have occasionally quarreled with Stephen's general estimate of the Deists. The consensus is that, for various reasons, Stephen underestimated their worth.[21] Obvious in *English Thought* is Stephen's contempt for the intellectual credentials of the Deists; moreover, he clearly objected to their want of taste in controversy. But, in his evaluation of their activities, he failed to recognize fully the effect of censorship upon their writing or that real danger faced those who dissented.[22] Consequently, the Deists, lacking the Victorian's freedom of controversy, were driven to present their arguments obliquely, hence with less effect. Perhaps, too, as one scholar has argued, Stephen's work was affected by his advancement of a favorite thesis: he found the optimism of the Deists unpalatable, and he noted in *English Thought* that those creeds which lacked recognition of human tragedy had little chance for survival.[23]

Stephen's interest in eighteenth-century thought was an offshoot of his fondness, dating back to his Cambridge days, for the literature of the period. By 1876, he had published fourteen essays treating eighteenth-century figures. Later the titles he contributed to Morley's English Men of Letters series were dominated by the period. Stephen's personal preference for the Augustan period happened to coincide with a general Victorian reassessment of the previous century which had begun in the 1870's. In his 1877 review of *English Thought,* Mark Pattison observed that, while the nineteenth century was still in reaction against the eighteenth century, it was beginning to be possible to achieve historical prespective.[24] The changing reputation of the Deists themselves is indicative of the larger shift in taste. From the time of Edmund Burke's 1790 assessment of them in his "Reflections on the Revolution in France" as men unworthy of further notice, the Deists were ignored until Mark Pattison's "Tendencies of Religious Thought in England, 1688–1750," in *Essays and Reviews* (1860), which treated them with respect. Pattison's essay inspired the major nineteenth-century account of the movement, Stephen's *English Thought.*

English Thought opens with an identification of a problem in the history of eighteenth-century ideas: from 1739 to 1752, David Hume published various aspects of his thought which was to become the watershed of English philosophy, but at this time few of his contemporaries recognized the significance of his work. Furthermore, theological speculation became quiescent in the second half of the century because of a pervasive skepticism. Stephen saw a causal connection. In a simultaneous process, ideas filter down from the best minds and gradually permeate the age, while, at the same time, the ideas themselves are powerful expressions of the tendencies of lesser minds. The second part of the process was to Stephen sufficient reason for the close examination of lesser minds of the age.

At the outset of *English Thought,* there is also a sane and sensible recognition of the usually loose connection between formal philosophic systems and the opinions of any age. Here Stephen took full cognizance of the extralogical factors which often shape men's ideas. He then turned around to examine the Deist controversy as a logical structure of argument for reasons which have already been noticed. His first task, however, was the establishment of the philosophic context. In general, he pictured the development of English philosophy in the eighteenth century as an empirical critique of continental a priori systems, especially that of Descartes; but he declined to locate the beginning of English empiricism in the thought of Francis Bacon. Instead, he began with Locke, moved forward to Berkeley, and then to Hume, for whom he had warm admiration. After Hume, Stephen noted the common-sense reaction to the Scotch philosopher's complete skepticism, as well as the materialism which emerged in the thought of men like David Hartley with his associational psychology. This latter development, as we might expect, was denounced by Stephen as representative of an untenable position because of its denial of rationality or mind. And, of course, he also observed the strongly rationalistic cast of the philosophy prevalent in the century at least until Hume.

Paradoxically, both the empirical and rationalistic tendencies in English philosophy reinforced the internal criticism of orthodox Protestant theology. Religion was submitted to two tests; the evidence of men's senses and the response of their rational faculties. After this development had occurred within theological circles, it was then picked up outside the establishment by those critics of orthodoxy who evolved the Deist position. Active during the first half of the century, the Deist movement then subsided, to be fol-

lowed by a period of relative intellectual inactivity which gave
place to the emergence of the historical mode of inquiry late in
the century.

In selecting the thought of Descartes for his philosophic point
of departure, Stephen's instincts were sound. He failed, however,
to apprise his reader fully of the tension which developed between science and religion—a story that has often been told
since.[25] For centuries there had been no quarrel. Medieval astronomy squared neatly with medieval philosophy and theology,
which were one and the same. Scholasticism—the synthesis of
Aristotle's pagan philosophy with the Christianity of St. Paul and
St. Augustine which was achieved by Thomas Aquinas in the thir-
teenth century—also had its cosmology, the geocentric Ptolemaic
system. Reason and revelation were both satisfied with a scheme
which put man's world at the center of the universe.

Then in the seventeenth century the science of astronomy became significant because of the invention of the telescope, and the
fixed universe of the Schoolmen was discovered by Galileo to be
in motion. His discoveries forced serious consideration of the
theories of Copernicus and Johann Kepler who had in succession
evolved a heliocentric view in the previous century. For some
poetic imaginations such as that of the English poet, John Donne,
the discovery represented a profoundly unsettling decay of the
universe. For philosophic minds such as the great French thinker,
René Descartes (1596–1650), the implication was that the senses
had betrayed the metaphysicians: the sun had only seemed to re-
volve around the earth. If neither the senses nor philosophic authority were to be trusted, how could certain knowledge of the
truth be attained? The epistemological problem led Descartes to
his method which was in turn to lead to an exaltation of man's
reason.

Suspicious of the data afforded the senses as well as of the answers of the Schoolmen, Descartes put all his trust in the ability of
his own reason. The mathematics so vital to Galileo's discoveries
provided him with a model of certainty in his investigation. Just
as mathematical propositions are true because, as Descartes and
other rationalists of the age saw it, they describe the objective
world, so, too, the mind must have certain innate ideas corresponding to that objective world. These ideas were to establish
their own validity by their very clarity, for to encounter them was

to accede to them. From the truths discovered in this fashion, an entire system was to be deduced as in mathematics. All of this system-making was to be accomplished without reference to sensory experience or authority. Descartes began with a provisional skepticism, resolving to doubt all that could be doubted; and the result was that he found himself left only with the certainty of the existence of the doubter—himself. Once the reality of the self was established, he then moved to an idea present to the self, God, an idea which Descartes argued was proof of God's existence since, as he held, no idea is present to the mind without some cause. The idea of causation itself thus became vital to the Cartesian system.

Returning to the self, Descartes intuited that the essence of the self, or the soul, was thought. The necessary opposite of the soul, that which does not think, is then matter, the essence of which is extension. Matter is, in other words, like a mathematical abstraction which is constant behind the varying forms our senses perceive in the world about us. The soul, God, and matter represent the three great substances of Descartes' metaphysical system, and they also represent the primary aspects of reality for Descartes. As he defined matter and soul, however, they represent mutually exclusive categories and an impossible gulf existed between them, for one cannot communicate with the other. Being nonmaterial, the soul has no basis for perception of matter. For Stephen this cognitive problem was a preposterous difficulty since modern science cannot exist on these terms. Men cannot learn of the laws of matter if their thought cannot communicate with matter. On the other hand, from Descartes' point of view as a religious person, the dichotomy was necessary. The theologian could continue to concern himself with the state of the soul; at the same time, the scientist could have complete freedom to discover the laws of the physical universe. The truths of each would in no way contradict the other. Furthermore, since Descartes had conceived the physical universe mathematically, its rationality as an object of scientific investigation was assured.

In Stephen's view, the pattern of English thought from Locke to Hume presented a picture of the triumph of man's intellect as it emancipated itself step by step from the murky systems of religious metaphysics, which, in one of his favorite phrases, represented "futile logomachies." Locke, who had first riddled Descartes' concept of innate ideas by his insistence upon referring all ideas to sensory data, had proved to his own satisfaction that the mind was innocent of ideas prior to sensory experience. As Stephen observed, however, the great philosopher was not without contradictions in his own thought.

As a philosopher, Locke maintained that the mind began as a blank tablet, but as a theological writer, he turned about to claim that, while man had no innate idea of God, a demonstration of his existence could be based on the idea of causality just as Descartes had done. Following Locke, Berkeley figured next with his critique of Descartes' theory of material substances, especially the process of abstraction involved in his description of matter. Developing Locke's position on the mind's subjective mode of perceiving matter in its secondary qualities, Berkeley found the idea of matter itself to be an abstraction, hence unreal. Yet both of these philosophers followed their empirical investigations while retaining at the same time their religious beliefs—a quaint inconsistency for Stephen.

It was left to Hume to achieve complete skepticism, one partly destructive of religious beliefs but one also hostile to reason itself. In Hume's demolition of the concept of innate ideas, the mind as well suffers, for it is reduced to a simple apparatus which receives impressions from the senses but lacks the faculties to evaluate them.

When Hume took up his philosophic inquiries, his principal task was to pursue the work of his predecessors to its logical conclusions. He accepted Locke's destruction of innate ideas as well as Berkeley's view of the process of abstraction. If the primary and secondary qualities taken from matter as abstractions are unreal because subjective, the remaining abstraction—matter—is itself unreal. Hume applied Berkeley's analysis to another of the substances, self or soul, with the same devastating results. Hume was less forthright with the third great substance, God. In fact, the debate still continues about Hume's true beliefs outside his study,[26] but for those with skeptical temperaments the implication was clear enough: belief in God was without foundation.

The logic of Hume's argument against the existence of innate ideas forced his denial of the complete adequacy of reason, and Stephen found this conclusion unacceptable. The Victorian rationalist was committed to the mind's ability to solve all human dilemmas with its logic. But the most dramatic aspect of Hume's thought was his demonstration of the invalidity of the important idea of causality. Such cause-and-effect relations as men think they perceive have no basis in reason. Those causal relations that men have become habituated to have in fact no basis in reason. The inference for the causal arguments for the existence of God employed by previous philosophers is clear. This implication was a clear gain to Stephen, but there was another edge to the Humian sword: it cut away the logical basis of science. If there were no logical basis for causality—such as a rational universe which would validate the scientist's belief that certain observed physical phenomena possessed causal connections which once discovered could be used to predict similar phenomena in the future —what was the future of science? Such an inference was completely unacceptable to Stephen.

In Stephen's critique of Hume's attack on causation, he had the good sense to avoid Mill's circular argument for uniformity in nature. But without it he was reduced to making a simple assertion of his own rationalistic belief in the regularity of nature. Furthermore, in the manner of the Victorian theologians he condemned, his assertion was unsupported by demonstration. Hume's position "implies the existence of chance as something more than a name for our ignorance, and must therefore be denied by all who (on whatever grounds) believe in the validity of reason, or the correlative doctrine of the regularity of the external world." Or:

Every phenomenon is known as the sum of a set of relations. The total phenomenon . . . is the effect. The separate factors . . . each of which is decomposable into various groups of relations to the perceiving subject, and to each other, are the causes. The same phenomenon can always be resolved into the same causes. If the phenomenon differs, some one or more of the components must differ. In this sense the assertion of the uniformity of causation is resolvable into something like an identical truth, or at least a statement of the postulate implied in all reason, and which constitutes the very reasoning process, that we can make identical propositions in identical cases. (*Thought*, I, 44)

Stephen's rationalistic orientation is evident here.

With Hume, the British criticism of Descartes was complete; for he had achieved "the final destruction of the old assumptions by which philosophers, developing and modifying the earliest modes of conception, had reconciled the doctrines of the regularity of the universe and the validity of reason with the observation that all phenomena are incessantly changing, and that knowledge of the visible universe can only be derived from the impressions made by the changing phenomena on the senses . . . the conceptions of God, the soul and matter were not destroyed, but they were transformed" (*Thought*, I, 45–46). Stephen's development of the empirical sequence in eighteenth-century philosophy is in essence, then, less a philosophical history than an impressionistic rendering of the history of ideas which highlight those developments tending to the destruction of any rational basis for religion.

The negation of rationalistic thought implicit in Hume's philosophy had its corollary: the resulting necessity for reliance upon experience. The impetus thus given empiricism resulted in the emergence of the historical method during the second half of the eighteenth century, although in Stephen's opinion the first results in the histories written by Hume, Robertson, and Gibbon were "crude." He saw their principal weakness to be their want of any philosophy of history which might have given their work unity by subduing events to a more subtle scheme than mere chronology. Such a weakness, said Stephen, was inherent in Hume's philosophy, especially as regards causation. The historical method had yet to mature in the work of Adam Smith and Edmund Burke.

Stephen concluded his sketch of the philosophic basis of eighteenth-century thought with yet another reminder that the truth or falsity of systems does not finally decide their effect upon the opinions of an age: "This or that creed may be proved or confuted to the satisfaction of logicians; if it cannot stand that test, its vitality is feeble; but it must also be capable of impressing the imagination of the ignorant and the stupid, or it will remain an esoteric doctrine—a germ, it may be, capable of bringing forth fruit under some new social conditions, but not, for the time, capable of becoming an important factor in the intellectual development of the race" (*Thought*, I, 60). Stephen also anticipated his explanation of the short life of the Deist movement: that its appeal for men's emotions was slight. Earlier in *English Thought* he had announced that "no creed . . . has a widely spread or continuous vitality which has not embodied all moods of the human mind. Sheer optimism is the least vigorous of beliefs" (I, 13). Deism, as we have already seen, failed to take cognizance of man's instinct for tragedy.

Following Mark Pattison's view of the Deist movement, Stephen divided his account of it into two almost concurrent phases: The first, "Constructive Deism"; the second, "Critical Deism." The second term was capacious enough to include David Hume and some atheists. Writers of the first movement, which lasted through the first half of the eighteenth century, questioned the reasonableness of miracles; those in the second stage employed an early and crude mode of historical inquiry to ask if miracles had really happened. The minds of these Deists were happier with a religion which they derived by reason from the natural world rather than with a religion which depended upon the revelation of the Bible. Stephen, who found the roots of Deism in the seventeenth century, described the movement as an offshoot of the Protestant revolt against the authority of Rome. In this century the conflict between authority and toleration sharpened after Englishmen saw the bloodshed that religious differences could produce. This tension was illustrated by contrasting the position of the French-Catholic Bishop Bossuet who stressed the authority of the pope with the pleas for toleration in John Milton's *Areopagitica* (1644) and in John Locke's *Essay* (1689).

Historically, the Protestant attack on Rome had first emerged as a moral revulsion, and it had then assumed a more intellectual cast as it denied the validity of the pope's position. The assault substituted the authority of the Scriptures for the pope, thereby setting a precedent for the subsequent displacement of the new authority, which was itself to be shouldered aside by the individual's reason in the Deist movement of the eighteenth century.

It appears that, once authority is successfully challenged, men find it difficult to stop short of anarchy—a fact which we of the twentieth century are painfully reaffirming. For the present, at least, it seems that the instincts of the seventeenth century as Stephen described them were not so very wrong. In that century men saw no middle ground between the alliance of philosophy and theology and "universal scepticism." If we deny "this central truth," the result is that truth is lost in a world which is a "blind congeries of shifting and changing forces (*Thought*, I, 17). At least in the latter half of the twentieth century, truth for many has become more than ever personal and subjective.

In *English Thought* the first theologian whose thoughts suggested the later paths of the Deist movement was the Anglican divine John Tillotson (1630–94), Archbishop of Canterbury, who argued against Rome in his *Rule of Faith* (1666).[27] His attack on the doctrine of transubstantiation, which he found to be contrary to the evidences of his senses, later provided Hume the basis of his *Essay on Miracles* (1748). Tillotson's rationalism was evident in his statement that no theological point could be established without an argument more cogent than the logical difficulties presented by the position. Reason had begun to take precedence over faith. Arguments similar to Tillotson's directed by other Protestants against the authority of Rome were subsequently to be turned against faith itself. Freethinkers in the next century would acknowledge Tillotson as a pioneer. Infatuated with their own intellectual powers, theologians began to treat Christianity as a subject for demonstration by the human mind. Less and less were they to regard it as a body of belief which had given human existence meaning for centuries.

The problem faced by these theologians was, as Stephen put it, "how to reconcile the ancient with the modern order of thought. How was the God of Christian tradition to be identified with the God of abstract reasoning?" (*Thought*, I, 69). Not only had orthodox conceptions of the cosmos been challenged by the new astronomy, but the traditional age of the earth itself was being questioned. Milton used the usual six thousand years for his *Paradise Lost*. A contemporary, Henry More, the Cambridge Platonist, had sung not only of an infinity of worlds in his poem *Democritus Platonissans* (1646) but of infinite space and time as well. Henry Power in 1664 postulated a twenty-thousand-year duration for the earth. And, in the next century, Georges Louis Leclerc, Comte de Buffon, in his *Histoire et Théorie de Terre* (1744), argued for a duration of at least seventy-five thousand years from the beginning of the Creation to the eighteenth century.[28] Such expansions of the concept of time were also to trouble orthodox commentators. The Deists had an answer: religion was to be based upon those ideas which were agreeable to human reason. Man's reason had but to consult the wonderful mechanism of the physical universe to see the work of the Creator.

The initial phase of the Deist movement which Stephen labeled "Constructive Deism" centered its debates on one question: can man's reason agree that Christian doctrine supplies something necessary to human nature? The particular occasion was Locke's "Reasonableness of Christianity" (1695) in which, putting aside centuries of biblical exegesis, Locke approached the New Testament on his own. He came to marvel at the essential harmony of the text as well as its truth and utility for man. He then jettisoned a vast cargo of theological dogma, and he concluded that the Christian need only accept Christ as the Messiah and that subscription to the Thirty-nine Articles of the Church of England, for instance, was but a human addition to the faith. From the acceptance of Christ, Locke held, every man's reason could lead him to a sufficient understanding of Christ's teachings. Thus, while deeply religious, Locke's book was at the same time a clear challenge to the orthodox establishment.

Because Locke's position implied a toleration of all sects, it naturally led to the question of Christianity's own validity. Why should men be Christians? Locke's rationalistic answer argued the utility of Christianity. He observed that, while the philosophers of the ages had formulated most of the moral values of Christianity, Christ had unified these and presented an authoritative and perfect moral system. It was, moreover, a system whose theories had been rendered meaningful by Christ's love for mankind, and the concept of a life after death was warranted by the miracle of his resurrection. In short, it was a religion which, unlike abstract philosophy, would reach the hearts of men.

Stephen dutifully summarized the dreary succession of debates which followed, as Locke's version of Christianity was developed by the Deists antagonistic to the established church and as theologians within the establishment replied. The end product of this particular phrase of the Deist movement finally appeared in a book called *Christianity as Old as the Creation* (1730) by an Oxford resident, Matthew Tindal. Tindal delineated more clearly than ever before the problem of a historical religion:

God is the creator of this vast universe; the Almighty Creator and Ruler of mankind, the source of all wisdom, the supreme legislator from whom all morality derives its sanctity, the inscrutable Being whom all men more or less dimly acknowledge in their hearts. Do we, then, render befitting homage to this august conception when we identify the God of reason with the God who selected a small, barbarous and obscure tribe in one corner of the earth as the sole recipients of his favour; when we declare that he imposed upon them a number of frivolous and absurd laws, or gave them commands which shock our sense of justice and humanity; when we hold that he allows a favoured class of mortals like ourselves to enjoy a monopoly of his grace, which they may retail to their humble followers; reveals to them the sole knowledge of the mysteries of his nature, and damns to everlasting torment all who by ignorance or misfortune are disqualified from receiving their magical privileges? (*Thought*, I, 114–15)

Stephen's own conviction adds heat to his summary of Tindal's deism. Furthermore, the implication of some of Stephen's word choices is more congenial to a Victorian agnostic than to Tindal as Stephen otherwise represented him. Such an identification of the God of reason with the God of Moses was unacceptable to Tindal, who felt that man's reason was adequate for the discovery of the necessary elements of true religion. Man had but to apply his faculty of reason to nature, both his own nature and the physical universe, both of which follow natural law as enacted by God. Revelation, miracles, and the priesthood could all be dispensed with in Tindal's eyes. Those who disagreed with Tindal mostly admitted the theoretical efficacy of reason but pointed to its obvious failure in practice.

Tindal's work concludes the "constructive" phase of Deism—the attempt to supplant orthodox Christianity with an abstract religion based on metaphysical demonstration. After Tindal, the movement loses momentum. As for why it did, Stephen's answer, as we have seen, was the "internal weakness" of Deism. More particularly, natural religion ignored a basic human need: its facile optimism, Pope's "whatever is, is right," ran counter to man's sense of tragedy. As Stephen explained it, "A purely optimistic creed always wants any stamina; for the great stimulant of religious emotions is a profound sense of the evils of human life" (*Thought*, I, 143). A sociological factor which would have been consistent with Stephen's introductory remarks in *English Thought* may also help to explain the phenomenon: Deism found its strongest adherents among "gentlemen," the aristocracy and educated churchmen, and it thus had no real exposure before the masses. But its abstractions would have been largely meaningless anyway, as Stephen continually suggests.

The other wing, "Critical Deism," had simultaneously mounted a frontal attack on Christianity which culminated in the skepticism of Hume's famous *Essay on Miracles*. Stephen's introductory remarks reflect a supercilious pity for both the Deists and the defenders of orthodoxy. In his eyes, this phase of the debate was characterized by a sense of unreality and futility since both sides were largely unaware of the historical method requisite for discussing the subject. His characterization of the opponents clearly conveys his tacit assumption that, despite the bungling of both sides, the horse they were beating—Christianity—was dead. It would be many years before he discovered his mistake. In the meanwhile, the assumption gave him Olympian detachment:

Whilst we smile at the errors, let us gratefully acknowledge the courage of the men [the Deists], who, with little learning and insufficient ability, began to break down the ancient superstition. Nor let us be slow to acknowledge that the defenders of the established order were animated for the most part, not by a cowardly fear of consequences, but by a genuine love for truth and for religion, as they conceived it. If the conceptions of these writers are cramped and their learning obsolete, they contrast advantageously with many of their descendants in the vigour and candour of their reasoning. (*Thought*, I, 158)

Stephen apparently felt that Victorian biblical criticism possessed finality and was therefore immune to obsolescence. Archeological events of the twentieth century, such as the discovery of the Dead Sea scrolls, have since shown the limits of Victorian knowledge.

In the eighteenth century a growing awareness of the hitherto unsuspected dimensions of secular history which was revealed by greater knowledge of other cultures was not without its impact upon the sacred history found in the Bible. Deists devoted their main energies either to criticism of those Old Testament prophecies which anticipated the coming of Christ or to criticism of the miracles associated with Christ's life. The arguments of the critical wing of Deism are characterized by a new ingredient: coarse humor. Stephen's remarks on this subject are anticipatory of the celebrated essay on the comic spirit by Stephen's good friend, George Meredith, which first appeared as part of a lecture the year after the publication of *English Thought*. Among other things Stephen said, "When a phantom dogma persists in haunting the living world, a laugh will cause it to vanish more rapidly than the keenest logical slashing" (*Thought*, I, 157). Despite his own ideological interest in the debate, Stephen deplored the low taste of some of the Deists' humor.

Oracles of Reason (1693), the work of Charles Blount, a follower of Lord Herbert of Cherbury, first evidences a tentative skepticism toward miracles, particularly in the Old Testament, and especially the story of the Fall of Man. This thrust was quickly parried by a churchman, Charles Leslie, with *A Short and Easy Method with Deists*. Leslie's method was based on what he considered to be four practical rules of evidence. By these rules he tested and validated the Old and New Testaments. Stephen's amusing and finally fair summary of the method was, "The difference between me and other people is that my records are true and theirs are not" (*Thought*, I, 167).

The criticism slowly gains momentum with Anthony Collins, a personal friend of Locke's. His approach reflects the timidity of the early Deists. He managed an indirect attack on the literal truth of the Scriptures by substituting allegorical interpretations in the manner of the early Church Fathers, but his motive was different. His *Discourse of Freethinking* (1713) was evidently intended to comfort other freethinkers by describing the movement as widespread. Ecclesiastics such as Bishop Tillotson were cited to support his position. He also stated the rationalist case in two propositions: first, the necessity to achieve sound belief through freedom of inquiry; second, the fact that such freedom leads to a denial of revealed religion. Collins excited the wrath of one of the great Cambridge scholars of the age, Richard Bentley (1662–1742), who crushed the unfortunate Collins with a contemptuous book. Almost simultaneously the greatest satirist of the age, Jonathan Swift, leveled his heavy artillery in *Mr. Collins' Discourse of Freethinking, put into plain English, by way of abstract, for the Use of the Poor*. Stephen's admiration for the Swiftian humor is obvious, but he described the essential argument as one from misanthropy: "All men are fools; therefore freethinking is an absurdity" (*Thought*, I, 177).

The debate quickly becomes more specific when Collins, after a time of involuntary retirement in Holland, took a turn at the argument from the standpoint of prophecy in his *A Discourse of the Grounds and Reasons of the Christian Religion* (1724). His position was that, while the Old Testament prophecies were the only real validation of Christianity, the only plausible demonstration of the fulfillment of the prophecies relied upon an allegorical mode of interpretation which allowed them to mean anything the commentator wished. The argument which validated Christianity from its miracles shortly came under fire as well. Thomas Woolston, another Cambridge man whom Stephen suspected to be mad,[29] took the position that the accounts of the miracles in the New Testament were themselves allegorical. Woolston's approach was more directly skeptical than Collins' had been, for he attempted to deny the death and resurrection of Christ himself. The coarseness of his method led Stephen to picture him as "a mere buffoon jingling his cap and bells in a sacred shrine; and his strange ribaldry is painful even to those for whom the supernatural glory of the temple has long utterly faded away" (*Thought*, I, 195). The response of the orthodox was weakest in Woolston's case; for descending to his level, they argued the case item by item, then concentrated on a demonstration of the truth of the resurrection with arguments like that of one church man who stood on the historical validity of the accounts of the apostles.

The final phase of the debate was signaled by two works which appeared in 1748: Hume's *Essay on Miracles* and Conyers Middleton's *Free Inquiry into the Miraculous Powers which are supposed to have existed in the Christian Church through several successive ages*. Earlier, Middleton had noted similarities between Catholic ritual and pagan religious observances. In *Free Inquiry* he focused attention on the division between the time when Christianity was witness to miracles and modern times when miracles are no more. His tactic was to attempt to move modern times back as far as possible: "Why, he asked by insinuation, should you believe Moses or Matthew if you won't believe St. Augustine? Why, if you believe St. Augustine, do you disbelieve modern stories of miracles and witchcraft?" (*Thought*, I, 227). His technique was to attack the veracity of the early Church Fathers, alleging widespread lying, gullibility, and intentional fraud. He contended that eighteenth-century man had the right to test Christian narratives in the same way that secular history was beginning to be examined.

Middleton's idea of applying the historical method to the subject of religion prepared the way for Edward Gibbon's famous *History of the Rise and Fall of the Roman Empire*, the first volume of which appeared in 1776. In Stephen's opinion, Middleton was the most effective challenger of orthodoxy among the Deists as well as the soundest thinker of Critical Deists; however, the philosopher Hume was not to be shrunk into a mere theological controversialist. The general consequence of the entire Deist movement was a dilution of English religious life until the appearance of John Wesley. As a result of Stephen's own special interest in the century, the apparent success of skepticism was satisfying. The emergence of a crude manifestation of the historical method was equally meaningful since he was confident that the more sophisticated Victorian application of the method would soon result in complete destruction of religion.

The most vivid writing in the first volume of *English Thought* is to be found in the two chapters which treat Bishop Butler and David Hume. For very different reasons, Stephen's emotional commitment is strong in both cases. While we would expect him to be critical of a theologian of the orthodox stripe, one aspect of Butler's thought held a powerful appeal. In his survey of an age of facile optimism, Stephen was drawn to a cleric who possessed a strong sense of the evils of human existence. As we have seen, Stephen was convinced that a viable creed had necessarily to be grounded on a tragic sense of life. The emotional appeal of Hume was both to be found in his fearless logic and in the candor of his expression of its results. In the jargon of the twentieth century, Hume was Stephen's "culture hero." Victorian intellectuals could profit from the example of the forceful Scotch philosopher.

The Analogy of Religion, Natural and Revealed, to the Constitution and Course of Nature (1736) by Joseph Butler (1692–1752) was perhaps the fullest and most philosophic response of the orthodox to Deism. Its timing also suggests that it was more directly a reaction to the ideas of Tindal. The moral earnestness of Butler drew the sympathy of Stephen, who found the bishop superior to Hume in this one respect. As Stephen saw it, in an age of optimism the deepest thinkers should be pessimists. Stephen's judgment of Butler has been sustained by modern critics, for the tendency is to regard him as the most impressive of the eighteenth-century English moralists. While his principal argument in the *Analogy* is as dated as the Deist controversy itself, his tragic sense commends him to twentieth-century readers.[30]

Yet the unbelief of Hume is triumphantly offered by Stephen as an antidote to the belief of Butler, for Hume shows what reason can do to the cloudy vaporings of the priests. Hume's writings are too well known to require further comment, but several aspects of Stephen's presentation are significant to this study. First of all, he was greatly relieved to be able to deal with that part of Hume's thought which he regarded as a pure rationalism uncontaminated by doubts as to reason itself. The well-known paradox of Hume's application of rationalistic analysis to theology after having denied reason's credentials was made a virtue by Stephen. As we have already noted, Hume had first argued that reason cannot show us order in nature; he then used this unproved order of nature's laws to deny miracles. Stephen tidied up the reputation of the great philosopher in this way: "His scepticism in metaphysics seems at times to be but half sincere, as scepticism must be which not only disputes certain dogmas, but throws doubt upon the validity of the reasoning process itself. The so-called scepticism of the theological essays is not in this sense sceptical; it admits the validity of our belief in the invariable order of the universe. His theological writings are made more cogent by admitting that fundamental truth" (*Thought*, I, 264).

Evidently arbitrary statements were not troublesome when it was necessary to advance Stephen's own causes. The same habit of mind is to be seen in his use of Kant's philosophy to structure the Hume chapter in *English Thought*. Kant is admissible as long as he shows that theology is outside the realm of pure reason; but, when his practical reason suggests the noumenal world of values which includes the idea of God, he is guilty of prejudice. Bias to Stephen is apparently but the flaw of anyone with theological leanings.

While admirable for its lucid grasp of the logic of the philosopher's attack upon miracles, and hence upon religion itself, Stephen's presentation is somewhat misleading as to Hume's principal role in eighteenth-century philosophy. Hume is commonly thought to have served a larger philosophic function than generating theological skepticism, and Basil Willey's view is representative. Thinkers of the age, having pushed abstract reason to its limits, needed the healthy example set by a philosopher who employed this same reason to demonstrate its own inadequacy.[31] Stephen's own rationalism led him to play down this antirational tendency. Yet later, when he dealt with eighteenth-century moral philosophy, he found that Hume's empirical or descriptive ethics, though of course anything but rationalistic, fell in neatly with his own love of what he took to be the scientific method. Hume's ethical theory in fact provided Stephen a more concrete program for his *Science of Ethics* than did the congenial hints he had noted in Butler.

The final chapter of the first volume of *English Thought* recounts the theological developments of the last half of the century. These include William Paley and his argument from design, the Unitarianism of Joseph Priestley, and a section "The Infidels" which includes Hume as historian, Gibbon, and Thomas Paine. For various reasons, Stephen was largely unsympathetic to this latter group. For example, although impressed with Gibbon's application of a genuine historical method as he offered causal explanations of the decline and fall of Rome, and fully aware of the general worth of Gibbon's history, Stephen nonetheless manifested an obvious distaste for the historian. Carlyle's brilliant evocation of particular historical moments was probably in Stephen's mind as he objected to Gibbon's inability to bring the dead past to life. In Stephen's view, Gibbon's general literary skill was insufficient to offset this deficiency. Had Stephen consulted his own interests, instead of adhering to more purely esthetic considerations, he might have been more enthusiastic about Gibbon's work. Gibbon's other fault was shared by Hume: both of these men were regarded as the great religious skeptics of their day; yet they were almost smugly conservative in politics.

The second volume of *English Thought* charts intellectual typography which is better known than the Deist controversy: the course of eighteenth-century ethical, political, economic, and literary development. The analysis of the century's ethical speculation is sharply focussed by Stephen's question, "How could order be preserved when the old sanctions were decaying?" As many have since suggested, this question was an avant-garde formulation for English society at large in both the eighteenth and nineteenth centuries. Since I believe that most historians would agree that the church generally continued to provide the operative moral sanctions certainly until the time of *English Thought*, the question thus produces a measure of historical distortion.

The origin of the question for Stephen himself is clear enough in his agnosticism. In his view, the function of theology in providing sanctions for society's values was vital; therefore, what was to replace the church? It must also be granted that the problem had actually emerged in Deist thought. Thinkers of the age produced two major answers: the intuitionist and the utilitarian. These alternative theories were to compete for English acceptance for the balance of the century. Afterward, they became a vital part of the complex fabric underlying Victorian ethical thought.

While a full account of the two schools is rather involved, the basic differences may be simply stated. The moral sense of the intuitionist perceived directly what ought to be done in any particular moral dilemma. The difficulty he recognized was the mobilization of his will to act as he knew he should. As a consequence, he evaluated deeds in light of the doer's motives, and the presumption was that the doer had freedom of choice. The utilitarian, on the other hand, found it necessary to consult society to gather empirical data about what men called good and bad. He faced the dilemma of deciding *what* should be done, for his evaluation of particular acts was based upon the consequences of the act. The utilitarian ethic hence possessed deterministic possibilities; therefore, moral choice did not really lie with the individual. At least historically, society has been forced to apply sanctions to conserve the values it had agreed upon, thus limiting the choices of the individual.

In his account of the two schools, Stephen clearly aligned himself with the utilitarians, although he repeatedly labeled its eighteenth-century manifestations "crude." One scholar's view of the dilemma suggests that both may have their application: the utilitarian serves society's interests; the intuitionist, the individual's.[32] Aside from the logical conflict which a system-maker would be sure to note, the conflict between the values of the individual and society itself is no doubt inevitable in a democracy.

It will be recalled that J. S. Mill, the Victorian inheritor of the utilitarian position, was a major influence on Stephen during his Cambridge days. Furthermore, Stephen was planning his own version of utilitarian ethics as modified by Comte and Darwin (*The Science of Ethics*). He was, therefore, strongly committed to a favorable account of the utilitarian position; as a result, he committed several distortions. For example, he was handicapped in his task by his very great respect for the intuitionist Butler. The result was that among his remarks on Butler, while he admitted that moral questions were exceedingly complex for the bishop, he failed to note that Butler had used this stance to attack the crudity of utilitarian moral calculations.[33] Hume, too, had to be tailored to fit; for, while there is little question that Hume was clearly utilitarian in his ethical thought, he also demonstrated intuitionist tendencies which Stephen found it necessary to deemphasize in order to stress the logical development of the school. Despite these problems, in its careful development Stephen's account was far superior to other contemporary treatments of the topic. J. S. Mill, for instance, had covered the same subject something over twenty years earlier with a far more simplistic approach.[34]

For twentieth-century readers the most interesting sections of the chapter on political theory are probably those which contrast the statesman Edmund Burke (1729-97) with Thomas Paine and other "Revolutionists." In light of Stephen's commitment to an evolutionary view of history, his sympathy for Burke, as opposed to those dedicated to revolution, should be no surprise.[35] Paine, Priestley, and even Jeremy Bentham himself were all deficient in the historical sense: "They are absolutely indifferent to that conception of the continuity of the social organism which supplies the vital element of Burke's teaching" (*Thought,* II, 215). Stephen's sympathy as a liberal for the conservative Burke has puzzled some, but it follows logically from his appreciation of Burke's powerful intellect and his probity as a public figure during a shabby period of English politics. Furthermore, as we have seen, the historical method was the real touchstone of *English Thought.* Stephen's approbation of eighteenth-century intellects was based upon their relative awareness of the historical method.

Students of Burke are most often troubled by the inconsistency of his support of the American Revolution and his vehement attack on the French Revolution. Burke had been typically practical in the first instance and curiously impractical in the second. Prior to the decisive events of 1776 in America, Burke had led the attempts at conciliation. He had insisted upon the emptiness of English theories about the absolute right of England to govern the colonies, and he considered the administration of the colonies to be both irrational and unjust. These positions were the direct result of Burke's practical political sense. His sympathy for the abstract doctrine of equality—the "Liberty, Equality and Fraternity" of the later French Revolution—was limited to the idea that government should concern itself with the happiness of the governed, not with the happiness of those in power. His concept was derived from the success of the English in making social and political compromises during the eighteenth century.

As a result, Burke did not sense the much greater rigidity of the more authoritarian French society; in fact, Stephen admitted that Burke was ignorant of the real conditions in France. The events of the American Revolution presented no serious challenge to Burke's views, since the American expression of the doctrine of equality resulted from a gradual emergence of American autonomy. Burke's reaction to the French Revolution, however, which appeared in his *Reflections on the Revolution in France* (1790)— a reaction based on the fact that venerable institutions were swept away overnight—was violently emotional. And, as Stephen conceded, Burke was wrong to deny that the event was justified by the suffering of the common man in France.

But Burke's *Reflections* also contained an intellectual response consistent with many years of his thought. Stephen was sympathetic to Burke's estimate of the spirit of French rationalism which, beginning with Voltaire, had prepared the intellectual climate of the revolution. The optimistic faith of these rationalists gave them a vision: reason was about to bring forth the millennium by canceling all history. Burke found this concept absurd. He saw, instead, that it was a license for the excesses of the mob. The French expression of the doctrine of equality presented itself to Burke in Stephen's words as a "fanatical creed" which represented a simplistic solution "without reference to the primary data of the problem."

Stephen's own historical sympathies are evident in his summary of the intellectual differences which obtained between Burke and the French theorists:

In fact, the revolutionary ideas embodied the formal contradictory to that truth, the full appreciation of which was Burke's greatest title to speculative eminence, and which guided his wisest reflections. To him a nation was a living organism, of infinitely complex structure, of intimate dependence upon the parts, and to be treated by politicians in obedience to a careful observation of the laws of its healthy development. To them a nation was an aggregate of independent units, to be regulated by a set of absolute *a priori* maxims. (*Thought,* II, 211)

For similar reasons, Stephen was never entirely in accord with the
English Utilitarians, despite his general sympathy with their empiricism. Set against Burke, the revolutionists—Paine, Priestley,
and Godwin—simply represented an impulse which was destructive to the social fabric because of their blindness to the continuity
of history.

Stephen recognized, as Burke had not, those abuses which had
led to the French Revolution. He saw, too, the way in which the
French rationalist attack on the church—rendered hateful to
the masses by its affiliation with the aristocracy—had facilitated the
revolution. But Stephen, like other Victorians, was probably too
close himself to the "mad fool fury of the Seine" to recognize that
Paine in *The Rights of Man* (1791), his reply to Burke, symbol-
ized the legitimate historical principle, change, which comple-
ments Burkean continuity.[36] Stephen had also been misled as to
Paine's sincerity, a mistake which he later acknowledged; but
even so, Paine was a "fanatical dogmatist." His crucial services as
a journalistic popularizer of ideas current in that day were recognized, but he does not appear as an original thinker; this, is not
surprising in view of Stephen's emphasis on intellectual history.
Even the most partisan of rationalist historians, A. W. Benn, does
not see Paine as a philosopher.[37] However meager Paine's philosophy, simplified by Stephen to "Kings, like priests, are cheats and
imposters" (*Thought,* II, 222), it fell in admirably with the feelings of those who were ready for action.

Having traced the course of speculative thought, Stephen
turned to an analysis of the effect of philosophy upon the imaginative literature of the age. At the beginning of *English Thought,*
Stephen had admitted that ideas shaped history only when many
extralogical factors were favorable to their acceptance; but he
now observed that ideas moved men's emotions only when given
concrete form in imaginative literature. The mechanism by which
philosophic thought becomes available to creative minds for literary purposes apparently did not interest Stephen, although he certainly knew Matthew Arnold's explanation in his famous essay,
"The Function of Criticism at the Present Time" which was collected in Arnold's first series of essays (1869). To Arnold, criticism's function is "to know the best that is known and thought in
the world, and by in its turn making this known, to create a current of true and fresh ideas." The critic thus makes available the

ideas of the philosophers for writers who root their flesh-and-blood creatures in this intellectual soil. Literary synthesis must be preceded by critical analysis. As will be seen, this view of the critic's role was too exalted to square with Stephen's feelings about the intrinsic worth of literary criticism.

What interested Stephen more was the way in which sociological factors shaped literary expression. It has already been shown that Stephen had chosen to emphasize other matters in *English Thought*, for genuine sociological analysis was postponed until his *English Literature and Society in the Eighteenth Century* (1904). Nonetheless, Stephen gave at least general recognition to the changes in English society which were instrumental in shaping literary expression. As is well known, the social setting was characterized by the rise of a cultivated middle class which included a group of literary figures who managed increasing independence from aristocratic patronage. These were the essayists and critics like Addison and Steele, the satirists like Swift and Pope, and the novelists from Defoe to Fielding who were the toast of a new institution, the coffeehouse. Stephen's analysis of the literary phenomena of the period was twofold: first, he took cognizance of those literary figures whom he found typical of the age; second, he outlined the Romantic reaction which gained momentum through the century.

He accepted the Romantic complaint which pictured Augustan poetry as deficient in spontaneous feeling, a deficiency attributed to the philosophy of the age. The basis of poetry for the school of Pope had been the abstract Nature of natural theology which had proved to be too abstract and lifeless for the production of concrete and hence meaningful symbols. The exemplar of this poetry, Pope, in spite of his sensitivity and grace of expression had, for instance, produced the didactic and intellectual poem *Essay on Man* (1733–34) as a result of the rationalistic climate. Worse, the way in which Pope and his contemporaries utilized Classical literature for their inspiration accentuated the artificiality of their poetry. The practice of the ancients, nature methodized, was reduced to rules. The emphasis on form which resulted from Augustan concern with Classical esthetic values (balance, symmetry, and temperance in expression) was unsatisfactory to Stephen; for, under the influence of the Romantic theory of organic form, Stephen preferred that poetic form result from the poem's content.

Stephen illustrated the artificiality of the Augustans by means of Pope's understanding of Homer which appeared in his famous translation. Homer was thought to be the artistic inventor, not the recorder, of the mythology he chronicled. Furthermore, Pope held, Homer invented according to rules of correctness. As Stephen wisely observed, periods of great art seem to be characterized by sound instincts, while lesser periods attempt to supplement the weakened instinct by rules which ultimately kill spontaneity. In his breathtaking coverage, Stephen necessarily oversimplified. His *Pope* (1880) reveals a more subtle understanding of the poet and his age.

To the credit of the eighteenth century, Stephen remarked that a vigorous prose emerged. The subject matter and the vehicle for it were determined by the fact that Deism had discredited metaphysical inquiry and therefore devitalized poetry. Although this explanation is not entirely clear, Stephen's apparent assumption is that a valid metaphysics is necessary for poetry; as I have tried to demonstrate elsewhere,[38] the theory may at least have validity in the case of nature poetry. At any rate, Stephen held that, since poetry and the vast questions of metaphysics had lost their appeal for eighteenth-century men, writers necessarily turned to prose and treated man and the problems of his society. This necessity accounts for the appearance of moralists like Swift and Johnson who shared a sense of profound evil in human existence as well as contempt for the optimism of those like Pope.

Although the expression varied considerably, a didactic tendency was strong among the novelists from Defoe to Fielding. The literary container of their moralizing, the novel, had emerged in response to the need for a genre suited to treatment of the problems of daily life about which men possessed strong feelings. In comparison with modern scholarship, the explanation of the appearance of the genre is, as might be expected, extremely sketchy; but, in fairness to Stephen, it must be remembered that his assessment of the English novel as an important art form appeared at a time when Victorian critics were just beginning to treat the novel seriously. In the 1870's many critics considered the novel immoral; others regarded it as frivolous entertainment; still others defended it for its moral instruction. Henry James's claims for the novel as an art form in his "The Art of Fiction" were not to appear in *Longman's Magazine* until 1884, and it was not until the twentieth century that a full-scale sociological explanation of the rise of the novel appeared.[39]

A current which ran counter to the dominant pattern of rationalistic theology and Neo-Classicism in literature emerged during the century. The religious manifestation was Methodism, a dissent from the Anglican church, and Evangelicalism, a development within the established church. The literary manifestation was the Romantic movement. If it is recalled that *English Thought* deals primarily with the logical structure of thought in the age, it should be no surprise to find these countercurrents spoken of as "the extra-logical reaction." In the context of *English Thought,* the phrase represents the sort of value judgment we might expect from a rationalist who had chosen to ignore an important implication of Hume's famous remark, "Reason is and only ought to be the slave of the passions." Stephen found this statement paradoxical because it was antirationalistic, but it had generated another sort of paradox. It represents that aspect of Hume's philosophy which reinforced the empirical tendency of the eighteenth century and led to utilitarianism, while at the same time it became the foundation for the intuitionist position in ethics. Those cultural phenomena which failed to advance the rationalist cause did not always get equal time from Stephen.

Stephen's estimates of the two reactions, theological and literary, epitomize the strengths and weaknesses of the Victorian rationalist historian. Methodism and the Evangelical movement were presented as lacking sufficient intellectual fiber for long survival. Both possessed strong emotional components, and neither had a truly logical relation to the speculative thought of the century. Stephen admitted the services of the Evangelicals in the abolition of slavery, and he admired Wesley's personal force and integrity. But these new Puritanisms lacked the intellectual stature of original seventeenth-century Puritanism. And Stephen was unable to accept religion as an experience which has its validity in the psychological realm. As we have seen, faith was for Stephen a mathematical demonstration with a missing step.

The most important esthetic matter treated by Stephen in *English Thought* was the history of the word "nature" during the eighteenth century. Subsequent scholarship has identified a host of meanings for "nature" not noticed by Stephen, but his analysis opened the way. His feeling for the historical method facilitated

his awareness of the fact that, while the ages of Pope and Wordsworth both urged a return to nature, the concept had very different meanings for the two periods. Nature revealed to Pope an
abstract metaphysical God through the mechanics of the Newtonian universe and the gradation of the chain of being. Later,
the same nature inspired in Wordsworth a powerful feeling of
reverence for the universe viewed as an organic whole which led
to an immediate intuition of a pantheistic world view. A debt is
owed Stephen by the extensive twentieth-century treatments of
this influential concept in such works as A. O. Lovejoy's famous
essay "Nature as Aesthetic Norm" in *Publications of the Modern
Language Association* (1912), Joseph Warren Beach's *The Concept of Nature in Nineteenth-Century English Poetry* (1936), and
Basil Willey's *The Eighteenth Century Background; Studies on
the Idea of Nature in the Thought of the Period* (1940).

Despite the special pleading manifest throughout *English
Thought*, it must finally be granted that the work represents a
pivotal one about the eighteenth century. Just as anyone who
wishes to study the Deist movement would be remiss if he failed
to read Stephen's book, students of the critical reputation of the
eighteenth century cannot overlook Stephen's contribution to historical study of the literature of that period.

III   The Science of Ethics *and* English Utilitarians

The next book produced by Stephen which bears a loose relation to his career as a historian of ideas was one which grew directly out of *English Thought*. Searching for a moral authority to
replace what he considered a dead theology, Stephen turned to
science for the discovery of the necessary sanctions. His *Science of
Ethics* (1882) represents an attempt to improve upon the utilitarian ethics launched in the previous century by Hume. Stephen felt
that one simply needed to examine society to discover those
values which produced the greatest happiness. He saw society
through the assumption of the Social Darwinist, by whom Darwin's biology was transferred directly into social theory. As Stephen put it, "The theory of evolution brings out the fact that
every organism, whether social or individual, represents the product of an indefinite series of adjustments between the organism
and its environment." [40] Morality, then, "is a product of the social
factor; the individual is moralized through his identification with

the social organism; the conditions, therefore, of the security of morality are the conditions of the persistence of society . . ." (p. 45).

These conditions were summed up as the successful adaptation to environment, and a scientific account of the resultant morality was his object. He sought the empirical data of those moral qualities which, in his eyes, represented a workable response to the social environment. Without doubt, he carried his own ethical assumptions into the investigation. Otherwise, his assertion, "I can prove that unselfishness and all the qualities which require intellectual development are essential conditions of social welfare" (452), would have been less confidently put. After all, selfish acts have been known to benefit society at large.

Whatever the practical difficulties which attended the application of his method of ethical inquiry, the validity of the approach is a more serious question. Ethics is usually thought to be a normative rather than a descriptive discipline. A descriptive ethics is, then, a contradiction in terms. From this point of view, Stephen seems to have confused the "what is" with the "what ought to be." He thought that identification of the "what is" would somehow lead the "normally constituted man" to genuine moral instincts, or that "beyond the science of morality there is the art which depends upon it" (441).

Several problems are suggested by this approach. What is the "normally constituted man"? Apparently, he is a person with Stephen's own moral sensitivity; for, like Hume before him, he took himself to be typical. His ideas about the moral qualities vital to society's moral health were assumed to be universally accepted, despite the fact that his own ethical values were the product of a religious training which he felt was no longer a force in British society. Since moral qualities were not necessarily instinctive in all men, it was foolish to expect that all men would respond as he did to ethical data gathered from society. Thus the basic assumption of the *Science of Ethics* itself was faulty.

It is curious that a rationalist like Stephen would fail to conceive of the logical possibilities inherent in his approach. What happens when a society develops pluralistic and contradictory values? What then is the meaning of a descriptive ethics? Even before the twentieth century, there were moments in history when pluralistic values obtained. Stephen himself, in a description of

the Renaissance temper which he sought and failed to find in
George Eliot's novel *Romola*, showed awareness of at least one
such moment. At such a time in history, the observer who sets out
to create an ethical system based on an input of purely empirical
data may then find that his information cancels itself out and that
no system is possible.

In addition to fallacious assumptions, Stephen proved incapable of the scientific objectivity which he had hoped to achieve.
His ethical data were marked by the very cultural influence which
he tried to eliminate: the Christian ethics of the Evangelical training of his youth. He thought that he and other humane rationalists
like himself could evolve a scientific morality which society would
accept; indeed, they had but to consult their own sensitive reactions to the evils of the world. But he was quite unwilling to admit
the source of his sensibility or his values. In this respect, his agnosticism again negated his own strong sense of historical continuity.
In his ethics he was guilty of the same historical approach for
which he had criticized the French rationalists of the revolution.

But the most serious flaw of the *Science of Ethics* was that it
was not even truly ethics; it was rather a primitive sociology, the
period piece of a Social Darwinist. Such a study may have a temporary utility as an analysis of a stable society; but, as Stephen
admitted, his own society varied in a complex way. He also admitted that the social science of the day was totally inadequate to
explain social change, much less predict it. As he said, "Anyone
who should have prophesied the history of the present century at
its beginning with any precision would have had himself to fore-
see the course of science, the attitude taken by the greatest of
thinkers, the influence upon men's imaginations of new conceptions of the world, and to have traced out an incalculable series of
changes in the relations of classes, and to determine the effect of
all these changes upon the material conditions of existence." And
all of this would have had to have been accomplished by a discipline which, even in the 1880's, he regarded as "nothing more
than a collection of unverified guesses and vague generalizations,
disguised under a more or less pretentious apparatus of quasi-
scientific terminology" (20, 10). Yet the construction of a scientific
morality was so important to him that he went ahead anyway.

The principal contradiction of the work is one which is also to
be observed occasionally in twentieth-century thought. Stephen

was like those social planners who see moral values solely as the product of environment and at the same time argue that environment must be controlled to conserve values. Evidently they—who are somehow free from this environmental determinism—can decide which values are to be conserved. The major premise of *The Science of Ethics* had appeared earlier in *English Thought:* "the moral law is substantially a code of rules, worked out by more or less conscious experience, which express the most obvious conditions of general well-being . . . [it is] the necessary result of the conditions of existence" (*Thought*, I, 247). Although Stephen would have recoiled in horror, logically his descriptive ethics would have to admit as legitimate data the attitude of a small group of twentieth-century molecular biologists who deny the relevance of ethical theory as they speculate upon manipulating the hereditary mechanism to achieve ends which they themselves have selected.

The best comment upon evolutionary ethics came shortly after Stephen's book was published. Ironically, it was made by an important figure in the scientific camp—T. H. Huxley. In his Romanes Lecture of 1893 at Oxford, "Evolution and Ethics," Huxley attacked the Victorian tendency to support the idea of progress with the theory of evolution. He held that progress really depended neither upon accepting nor upon rejecting the evolutionary process but upon replacing it with an ethical system. He conceded that ethical ideas have evolved, but he denied that their evolution was related to biological evolution. Clearly, the survival of the fittest was not necessarily the same as the survival of the most just in the history of the world.

All in all, *The Science of Ethics*, despite Stephen's own high regard for it, is clearly his worst book. His loyal friend and official biographer, F. W. Maitland, found its dullness irritating. His other biographer, Noel G. Annan, considered it the work of an amateur and regarded it as a demonstration of the incompatibility of science and ethics.

The work which carried the story of English rationalism forward into the nineteenth century, *The English Utilitarians*, did not appear until twenty-four years after *English Thought*. A detailed account of this more specialized study is outside the interests of the general reader, but several of its characteristics demonstrate the growth of Stephen as a historian of ideas during the last part of his life. Generally speaking, *English Utilitarians* is more balanced and objective than *English Thought*. In his introduction, for example, Stephen granted that, while intuition and empiricism are representative of a basic antithesis in philosophy, both points of view have their own validity and application. This admission is typical of the work which derives its interest for the reader from lively history and biography rather than from a burning desire to proselytize for an ideology. Stephen's intervening labors on the biographies of the English Men of Letters series had not been without their effect. Compared with *English Thought*, the style is more pithy; it derives its strength from greater use of concrete imagery and from less reconstruction of logical argumentation. The account of the late eighteenth- and early nineteenth-century historical scene is also more substantial. For instance, Stephen attended to social and political problems like the industrial revolution and the slave trade as he had not in the earlier work.

Stephen's general concern was to show the intrinsic worth of the Utilitarian movement from Jeremy Bentham (1748–1832) to James Mill (1773–1836) and his son John Stuart Mill (1806–73), a group which emerged as better legislators than philosophers. Yet his treatment of the key figures of the movement reveals their general deficiency in imaginative sympathy, for the Utilitarian reduced life to an abstraction by considering people only as a part of the social machinery. To them, men's emotions were important only when manifested in conduct with social implications. Bentham was typical in that he assumed an eighteenth-century abstraction—Man—then ignored history to proceed deductively from this fiction to social legislation. The Utilitarians began by insisting upon experience and finished by making abstract assertions deduced rationalistically. And the logic of the Utilitarians was also defective. John Stuart Mill's *System of Logic* may have been one of the most important books of Stephen's undergraduate days, but its illogic was ruthlessly dissected in *English Utilitarians*.

Special aspects of the movement have been treated in greater detail in Emery Neff's *Carlyle and Mill* (1924), George Nesbitt's *Benthamite Reviewing* (1934), and Francis Mineka's *Dissidence of Dissent* (1944), but like *English Thought*, *English Utilitarians* cannot be avoided by anyone seriously concerned with the subject.

CHAPTER 4

Man of Letters

STEPHEN'S rationalism and his commitment to agnosticism had spurred him to writing which earned his distinction as a pioneer historian of ideas. At the same time, the pleasure he found in English literature motivated a more esthetic phase of his career which established him among the leading Victorian literary critics and biographers—a phase of his career that may prove to have been the more successful. His sincerity, dedication, and intellectual power are clearly evident as a historian. Yet the main thrust of his rationalistic writing was destructive. Although every age needs its doubters, men seldom build enduring reputations in this fashion; the Voltaires of history are few. As Stephen himself noted in his "Cynic" series for the *Cornhill,* the disparager's role is generally not an exalted one. On the other hand, when he devoted his energies to literature, his insights were more constructive and therefore probably more lasting. Though not a Matthew Arnold, he merits serious consideration as a pioneer critic of the English novel, as a leader in the Victorian rehabilitation of the Augustan age, and as one who early recognized the consequences of the social matrix for literature.

In general, the appearance of Stephen's literary criticism coincided with the chronology of his historical writing. But such a large bulk of his literary criticism and biographical work fell into the last twenty or so years of his life that this interest and work were clearly dominant. These final years were darkened by his failing health, which was first brought about by the incredible demands made upon his energies by the eight years of editing the *Dictionary of National Biography.* They were made desolate by the deaths of his close friends and family who dropped away one by one. But, to some extent, the bleakness of these years was offset by the recognition of his contemporaries. After Matthew Arnold died in 1888, Stephen became the most important Victorian man of letters. His editorial work on the *Dictionary,* his literary criticism, and his biographies brought him honorary degrees from Harvard, Cambridge, Oxford, and Edinburgh. Finally, he was knighted at the coronation of Edward VII in 1903. These honors, however, represent only the public part of his life.

Within the domestic circle, the children especially paid a dear price for Stephen's lifelong efforts to overcome his introverted, hypersensitive nature. As Professor Annan has verified, the portrait of Stephen by his daughter Virginia Woolf in her novel *To the Lighthouse* (1927) is an accurate rendering of a side of his personality not experienced by his intimates. Mr. Ramsay destroys the pleasure of his children's outing by insisting that, however much they may desire it, the row to the lighthouse will be a failure because it will rain. He also spoils the occasion in a more subtle way by presenting himself as a tragic figure to be pitied by his children. A thoroughgoing egotist, Mr. Ramsay wants his family to suffer with him. At the same time, his self-pity blinds him to the emotional needs of those closest to him.

In the world outside his family, Stephen manifested a gradual withdrawal from the nominal social life he had earlier experienced. To those who were not his intimates, he had often seemed austere. In Thomas Hardy's poem "The Schreckhorn" (1897), the poet associated the lofty, rugged grandeur of that forbidding peak in the Bernese Oberlands with Stephen's personality. Although Stephen's good friend John Morley had summed him up as "the most considerate and faithful of men," he had also admitted that those "who did not know Stephen often found him unceremonious and even grim, and in truth he did not suffer gladly either a bad argument or a fool in person." [1] Gradually, he became taciturn even with close friends. In the 1880's, James Russell Lowell recorded delightful visits with Stephen at his St. Ives retreat in Cornwall; but in the next decade, another visitor, Henry James, found but little conversation in long quiet walks with his host.

One of Stephen's greatest pleasures during these years resulted from his walks with the little band of his friends, the Sunday Tramps. Organized by Stephen in 1879, the Tramps were a peripatetic version of the Boston Saturday Club. Unlike the Metaphysical Society, the Tramps were men whose sympathies were closer to Stephen's own views. The sixty members of the group included prominent Victorian intellectuals such as G. Croom Robertson

(1842–92), philosopher and student of Thomas Hobbes and the first editor of the philosophic journal *Mind;* Douglas W. Freshfield (1845–1934), well-known mountaineer and geographer; Frederic W. Maitland (1850–1906), Cambridge professor of law and later Stephen's biographer; Robert Bridges (1844–1930), poet and later poet laureate of England; Nathaniel Hawthorne's son Julian (1846–1934), a popular novelist; W. P. Ker (1855–1923), famous Oxford professor and critic of medieval literature; and R. B. Haldane (1856–1928), a member of Parliament at the time, later a secretary of state for war, and also a historian of ideas. As the leader, Stephen demonstrated his personal force as a mover of men in physical enterprises, an ability which had evolved during his Cambridge years and in the Alps. Over 250 of these sorties which often exceeded twenty miles are recorded.

In 1891 Stephen's physical decline forced him to relinquish command of the Tramps. The previous year he had made his last voyage to the United States where he had visited his friend Lowell at Elmwood the year before the American died. In 1894, he made his last trip to his beloved Alps and returned to learn of his brother's death. The next year brought the heaviest blow of all— the death of his second wife, Julia. In addition to these losses, the last eight years of his own life were plagued by a deafness that reduced him to participating in the lives of his children only by means of an ear trumpet.

In view of his personal circumstances, Stephen's literary production during these last years is astonishing. After his health forced him to turn over the editorship of the *Dictionary of National Biography* to Sidney Lee in 1890, his publications included the biography of his brother Fitzjames (1895), the four volumes of *Studies of a Biographer* (1899), the three volumes of *English Utilitarians* (1900), *George Eliot* (1902) and *Hobbes* (1904) in the English Men of Letters series, and *English Literature and Society in the Eighteenth Century* (1904). He finally succumbed to cancer early in 1904.

I   *Development as a Literary Critic*

Stephen's performance as a literary critic is clearly understood only in the light of the general nature of the critical task as it evolved during the nineteenth century. The emergence of the English middle class as a political and economic force in 1832 was

accompanied by a need for the establishment of esthetic standards acceptable to that class. Neo-Classical principles of the previous century were in a sense tainted by their association with aristocratic patronage. Consequently, middle-class intellectuals began
to evolve their own esthetic. As various commentators on the period have noted, their esthetic was largely a moral one. Variations
on the theme—great art is produced by those with profound
moral visions—pervade the thought and practice of the important
Victorian artists and critics. Whatever beauty may be created, to
them the final end of art is to teach important human truths. And,
while such a view may strike the reader as "typically Victorian,"
he is reminded that, as Jerome H. Buckley has observed, such an
esthetic is hardly unique since it was grounded on the basic assumptions of most Classical esthetic theories.[2]

At the same time, the moral esthetic held a powerful appeal for
the middle class. The art critic, John Ruskin, for example, first
experienced a phenomenal success largely as a result of his ability
to explain painting and architecture in terms acceptable to the
middle-class reader. Although Ruskin's esthetic was dominated by
moral and religious considerations, his position developed from
about 1840 to 1860 to include the psychological, social, and political implications of art for his countrymen. As he grew more critical of English society, especially of the ills created by rapid indus-
trialization, his message became less palatable to his countrymen.
His criticism hearkened back to the Middle Ages when, as he saw
it, a sound society allowed whole men to create great architecture.
Despite its efficiency, the division of labor in an industrial society
destroyed the worker.

Victorian literary criticism itself dealt increasingly with the relationship of literary art to its roots in society, and such an approach often led to the criticism of society. Matthew Arnold's
view of poetry as a criticism of life, for example, was extended in
his own practice to delineate the functions of the critic whose
province included both the interpretation of literature and the critique of society. Arnold's love of Classical literature led him to
compare the ancient Greek's feeling for beauty with the lack of
imagination and the smug materialism of his own class whom he
attacked as "Philistines" in *Culture and Anarchy* (1869).

Stephen himself assumed the additional burden of eighteenth-
century scholarship in addition to the dual role of social and liter-

ary critic. The first result should be an appreciation of the fact that Stephen was handicapped both by having, to a considerable extent, to function as a scholarly pioneer, and by assuming the dual role of social and literary critic. The neglected state of eighteenth-century studies and criticism of the English novel made the first inevitable, but the second handicap was, perhaps, a mistake of judgment. If so, it was a common one in the Victorian period, as is illustrated in Arnold's own career. At any rate, Stephen's task was enormous but worthwhile. Stephen began with general evaluations of eighteenth-century novelists, then worked out the intellectual history of the period in *English Thought,* expanded the subject with biographies of key Augustans, all the while continuing to develop an esthetic theory which would be relevant to Victorian fiction.

The corollary of this development as a literary critic was an increase in his objectivity as a critic of society, a development which we have observed. Basically, the task of the scholar was apparently more congenial to Stephen than some aspects of the literary critic's domain—especially that of poetry. While he showed real skill in vivifying abstract ideas as an intellectual historian, his analysis of poetry revealed far less discrimination than that of his famous contemporary, Arnold. The comparison of the two as critics began with Stephen's friend, John Morley, who regarded Arnold as the more cosmopolitan and able in his examination of the relationship between literature and its social background.[3] Although subsequent comparisons have continued this view, the fact that Stephen is compared with the foremost critic of the Victorian period suggests the intrinsic value of his criticism.

Stephen had met Arnold early in his London days, but the two men were never close friends, despite Stephen's early admiration of the older man, especially because of his brashness as a social critic. By 1884, a letter of Stephen's to his friend Norton reveals that he had begun to be irritated by the smugness he saw in Arnold's social criticism (Maitland, 380). He particularly resented Arnold's critical terminology, even though he later admitted in his essay on Arnold that the term "Philistine" was probably descriptive of himself—but we have already observed the dogmatism of Stephen's own social criticism. And the distance between smugness and dogmatism is surely not great.

After Arnold's death, Stephen delivered a lecture on the poet in

1893, one later reprinted in Volume II of *Studies of a Biographer,* in which he expressed strong approbation of Arnold as a poet and as a literary critic. Stephen was particularly impressed by the soundness of Arnold's critical intuitions. Arnold's poetic sensitivity, which made him surer and more graceful in his criticism, caused him to select passages from the great poets as touchstones in his criticism in a way superior to Stephen's; and the younger man's essay on Arnold reflects his own awareness of this superiority. Indeed, Stephen described himself as having a prosaic mind when compared with the poetic sensibility of Arnold. The difference in their imaginations is suggested by the historical periods to which they were most strongly attracted: Arnold found Hellenic grace congenial; Stephen preferred the common sense of the Augustans.

Is Stephen to be considered Arnold's disciple?[4] He often follows Arnold in his feeling that the critic is to judge and rank literature, but in his essay on Arnold, Stephen stated that the function of the critic was simply to "distinguish between the sham and the genuine article";[5] it was not to rank writers in a hierarchy. In this respect, Stephen is closer to appreciation than judgment. Still, as we shall see, the net effect of Stephen's criticism of the English novel was to help to bring order out of chaos. Although Stephen certainly accepted Arnold's opinion that great literature functions as a criticism of life in the largest sense, Stephen's criticism concentrated more on the moral quality of the writer and less on purely esthetic aspects of his work than did Arnold's. However, a close examination of Stephen's moral esthetic reveals that it does not differ essentially in kind from Arnold's own.

In our century a continuing debate over Stephen's merits as a critic also illuminates the general nature of his performance. The debate began with a quarrel between two English critics, Desmond MacCarthy and Q. D. Leavis. In his undergraduate days MacCarthy had been an acquaintance of Leonard Woolf, later the husband of Stephen's most famous daughter, Virginia. In those days MacCarthy was also an intimate of the Stephen family, and in 1937 he criticized Stephen as deficient in esthetic standards. Because Stephen's response to literature was also too intellectual, it lacked emotional depth. MacCarthy further asserted that Stephen's criticism was impaired by his moralistic approach, his rationalism, and his failure to regard literary criticism as a kind of creativity. MacCarthy, who represents the impressionistic and personal response to literature in English criticism, writes criticism that is appreciative, not judicial. Rather than attempting to establish a hierarchy of artists, he stresses the uniqueness of the writer's personal vision; he prefers also to emphasize the writer's ambiguity of statement instead of his moral gravity.

MacCarthy was answered two years later by Q. D. Leavis who shared Stephen's belief that the critic must proceed with a systematic appraisal. To her, Stephen's rationalism was not a weakness but a strength, particularly when he employed it to examine the moral sense and general philosophy of a writer. In short, Mrs. Leavis regarded Stephen as a judicious critic who was bound to document his pleasure in a writer's work by demonstrating his moral seriousness, his intellectual depth, and his craftsmanship. Her defense linked Stephen with Henry James because of the concern for the moral seriousness of the writer which they both reflect in their work.[6]

In 1951, Stephen's second biographer, Annan, sought a middle ground and demonstrated both the strengths and weaknesses of his subject. He appreciated Stephen's accomplishments as a judicious critic, but he finally granted Stephen's failure to subject the novel to the close technical analysis customary in our century. Fourteen years later René Wellek, who amplified MacCarthy's position, insisted that Stephen was seldom aware of esthetic criteria; instead, he had judged literature on intellectual and moral grounds. Furthermore, the ethical values of Stephen were characterized by Professor Wellek as a narrow social morality, one essentially utilitarian.

I suspect that the Platonic triad—Truth, Beauty, and Goodness—which is implicit in Wellek's judgment may have unduly influenced his appreciation of Stephen's work. If criticism is extended beyond questions of pure form, some concern for the ends of art seems inevitable. In that case, certainly the intellectual and ethical aspects of a particular work of art also become relevant topics for the literary critic. It should be noted that Wellek praised Henry James for a concept of fiction which, to a considerable extent, parallels Stephen's idea that poetry might be assessed in terms of its implicit philosophy. The novel, to James, is vicarious experience which can lead the reader to self-knowledge because the artist has presented his own synthesis which, in the best writers, can be dignified as a philosophy. Professor Wellek justifiably saw in this the implication that the artist speaks not only as an esthetic man but also as one who is rational and ethical.

Stephen was also criticized by Wellek for his application of the sociological approach; it was deficient because his moralistic tendency prevented him from admitting the relativistic values of the method. Finally, Wellek doubted that Stephen as a literary critic had anything to say to the modern reader.[7] Although we find much truth in these remarks, I believe that they are not entirely fair to Stephen's achievements. His critical stance, despite its Puritan overtones, was more broadly humanistic than Wellek was willing to grant.

Stephen's seemingly cavalier attitude toward the practice of literary criticism is yet more deeply disturbing to modern commentators. In 1900, he said, "I always feel that a critic is a kind of parasitical growth, and that the best critic should come below a second-rate original writer" (Maitland, 455). A similar statement appeared in *English Literature and Society in the Eighteenth Century,* and it reflects an attitude toward criticism which from the first he held consistently. While the general reader may be sympathetic to this point of view, it represents a treasonable position to many professionals. Despite this apparent contempt for criticism, in 1876 Stephen defended the function of the critic in a *Cornhill* essay, "Thoughts on Criticism." [8] In it, he said the critic's business was to promote "a critical spirit such as raises instead of depressing the standard of literary excellence." Deploring the tendency of Victorian critics to assume that their personal taste corresponded to universal taste, he echoed David Hume's "Of the Standard of Taste" (1757) by insisting that individual taste must be validated by that of cultivated individuals with the passage of time. As he said of the critic, "The fact given him is that he is affected in a particular way by a given work of art; the fact to be inferred is, that the work of art indicates such and such qualities in its author, and will produce such and such an effect upon the world."

In theory, at least, Stephen seems to have the best of both worlds—judicious and appreciative criticism. As he explained the best stance for the delivery of judgments produced by his method, it is easy to see that his diffidence results from a very real sense of the hazards that attend the act of judgment. His ideal critic would avoid dogmatism through his recognition that he is but an individual speaking. On the other hand, his position, that "of a presumably cultivated individual . . . should give at least a strong presumption as to that definitive verdict which can only be passed by posterity." Such caution is refreshingly sane when we recall the occasional modern critic whose work suggests the feeling that criticism is more important than creative work, especially when his criticism is accompanied by the conviction of an invincible ignorance and an incurable want of taste on the part of the reading public.

In practice, Stephen is apparently more limited. His approach seems to be that of the typical mid-Victorian critic who demands moral instruction from art. When the exact nature of this moral instruction is clearly understood, however, Stephen is less parochial. He produced his most valid insights when he faced a writer who could profitably be subjected to ethical and rational scrutiny. He therefore preferred not to emphasize purely esthetic problems but, at the same time, did not deny their importance. It is hard to imagine the humanist of today who would be unable to sympathize with the spirit of a statement made by Stephen in 1881: "It is impossible ever really to exclude moral considerations from esthetical judgments; though it is easy to misapply them, or to overlook the importance of other aspects of a man's total influence. To make a poet into a simple moralist—a teacher of a certain definite code of ethics, is to put him into a wrong place, and judge him implicitly by an inappropriate criterion; but it is equally true that he can only be deprived of moral quality if he takes no interest in the profoundest and most comprehensive topics of human thought and faith." [9]

II   *The Moral Esthetic*

The *Cornhill* essays from 1868 to 1881 suggest that Stephen's esthetic position ranges from a narrowly didactic concept of art to a more broadly humanistic concern with literature as a vehicle of values. The latter view stems partly from Stephen's agnosticism, which led him to expect that religion would soon cease to conserve the values which he felt essential to society—an idea similar to Arnold's expectation that poetry would someday replace religion. The former, or didactic, concept derived from the Evangelical influence which led Stephen to consider literature as moral instruction, but at times it was complicated by a distrust of art itself.

The 1868 essays on Samuel Richardson and Daniel Defoe[10] established Stephen's concern with moral earnestness in fiction. As we have noted, such a quality derived from the author himself and was to be revealed in his work through indirection rather than by means of an openly didactic approach. The author's ethical orientation led him to select certain types of characters and to stress certain motivations. In Richardson's case, it was the source of his artistic achievements as well as of his failures. It led to his concern with feminine psychology and, at the same time, to the narrowly prudential quality of his ethics that hindered his artistic development of the subject. Defoe's characters reflected a similar flaw in that his moral vision limited his understanding of psychology to the extent that his characters were all variations of himself. Stephen's essays also revealed an ambivalent attitude toward the problem of verisimilitude in fiction. Actual illusion, Stephen felt, was not the goal of the novelist. At the same time, he praised both for their powers of observation which he inferred from the solidity of detail in the work of both—a quality which brought their stories closer to life.

Five years later Stephen's analysis of Edward Bulwer-Lytton's novels continued the attack on direct didacticism. He admired Lytton's idealism but found its expression to be too forthright; the result was that Lytton's work was "artificial" and lacked "spontaneity." Related to the tonal deficiency were more basic difficulties in the novels. Stephen found them overplotted and weak in characterization, as a consequence, he felt, of the author's lack of psychological understanding. The novels, he concluded, did not suggest "that penetrative imagination which goes down to the roots of character, and appreciates at their true value the forces of human passion." [11] While Stephen's concepts of fiction were hamstrung by his attitude toward verisimilitude, it is clear that he sought a kind of psychological truth in fiction. He was also capable of explaining why a particular piece of fiction was bad art.

One of the more comprehensive statements of his esthetic is to be found in "Art and Morality" (1875).[12] Angered by the development of the "art-for-art's-sake" movement of the esthetes of the 1870's, Stephen perhaps overreacted. Two years earlier Walter Pater (1839–94) had sung the joys of the purely esthetic outlook in the conclusion of *The Renaissance*. The intense appreciation of a moment of beauty in its own terms was paramount to Pater: "To burn always with this hard, gemlike flame, to maintain this ecstacy, is success in life." The implication that art could exist in an ethical vacuum drove Stephen into the most extreme statement of his own position: "If a man really has the impudence to say that immorality is right because it is artistic, he is either talking nonsense or proposing as a new law of morals what is too absurd to require confutation. . . . Morality is a system of rules for regulating our passions. Art is the means by which the men who feel most strongly and think most powerfully appeal to the passions of their weaker brethren. . . . Art provides the most powerful, though the least obtrusive, means by which the standard of morality is affected."

Stephen went on, however, to decry prudery and direct didacticism. The latter was "a blunder in art; but the blunder is not that they moralised, but that they moralised in the wrong way." Values should emerge through "vivid imaginative symbols" rather than through "abstract logical formulae." The poet and the novelist have their own distinct modes of expression which are not the philosopher's. Equally important is the soundness of the artist's character since art is to teach through the reader's identification with a "great and good man." Indeed, the very pleasure of literature for Stephen derived from the fact that "it brings the reader into contact with the best minds at their best moments."

Stephen's attitude toward poetry in "Art and Morality" seems especially limited. Poetry, he felt, "in every case, without exception . . . should stimulate the healthy, not the morbid, emotions. . . ." When, however, the meaning of "healthy" is clarified, Stephen is not so narrow as he seems. Elsewhere in the essay he noted that "all healthy phases of human feeling may be rightfully represented. Keats is not to be condemned because his poetry is the expression of a sensuous temperament. A keen delight in all external beauty of form and colour, even the lower pleasures of the animal appetites, may be fitly expressed in art." Seemingly a narrow Puritan in his criticism, Stephen, at his best, realized that literature must first please the reader. It could also convey a sense of the complexity of man's moral nature and the essentially tragic nature of his existence, but the artist's moral insights must first be fused with his imagination in the creative process.

Stephen is at his best as a critic in "Wordsworth's Ethics" (1876).[13] One explanation of his success is that the poet's work had assumed a special meaning for him after the crushing blow of the death of his first wife, Minny, the year before. As in J. S. Mill's own personal crisis which he recorded in the *Autobiography* (1873), Wordsworth's poetry satisfied emotional needs ignored by a purely rationalistic approach. Aware of his limitations, Stephen found a legitimate way to show his admiration of the poet. His praise of the poet's concern for the full and harmonious development of human faculties puts the essay in the humanist tradition which goes back to Plutarch's *Lives*. The tradition is illustrated in the novels of Stephen's friend, George Meredith, who developed the "Triad" of "blood, brain, and spirit" to epitomize a balanced human being. Writing twenty-six years after the poet's death, Stephen directed his attention to Wordsworth's ethical insights because "so much has been said by the ablest critics of the purely poetical side of Wordsworth's genius" (276). Clearly, Stephen admitted the importance of esthetic matters, but he just as clearly confessed his own inadequacy in handling them.

The essay blazed no new trails for the poet's reputation, since most mid-Victorian critics placed Wordsworth into the company of Shakespeare and Milton. And we are given nothing about the poet's development or such technical matters as language or symbolism. Absent, too, is a full account of the poet's pantheism and his mysticism; but these subjects were not congenial to Stephen. This essay is the product of a sensibility dominated by what Arnold would have called a "Hebraic tendency"—the stress on conduct—but one which is not blind to the Hellenistic tendency: the cultivation of intellect and pleasure in beauty. There is evident concern with the moral content of literature, but the approach here is humanistic; that is, the effect of literature upon the individual, rather than the social organism, is stressed. Furthermore, we find full recognition of the poet's sense of joy in nature.

In "Art and Morality" Stephen had asserted that "every poetry deserving the name implies the presence of certain modes of conception which only require systematic analysis to be turned into philosophy." In the Wordsworth essay, the analysis of a poet's work to discover his philosophy was justified as a consequence of the fact that poetry and philosophy are but two ways of expressing the responses of a serious person to the human condition. Both the poet and the philosopher direct themselves to the nature of man, his world, and the ethical consequences of such knowledge. The poet's method is intuitive, emotionally subtle, and symbolic; the philosopher's is demonstrative, logically consistent, and discursive. Both are at their greatest when their views are the most comprehensive. In 1889, Stephen made clear what philosophy meant to him: "Poets certainly 'don't live by systems.' Nor, for the matter of that, do philosophers. I think that a philosophy is really made more of poetry than of logic; and the real value of both poetry and philosophy is, not the pretended reasoning, but the expression in one form or other of a certain view of life" (Maitland, 396).

The critic who prefers to limit his inquiries by treating only the ways in which language and structure please the reader finds little to his liking in Stephen's approach. And the characterization of Wordsworth as "a prophet and a moralist, as well as a mere singer" certainly suggests a condescending attitude toward art. Perhaps, too, the content of this essay is more properly that of the historian of ideas rather than that of the literary critic. But, after such methodological disputes are recognized, it is clear that the essay still contributes to an understanding of the poet's work.[14] One likely reason for its continued appeal is that Stephen's esthetic views are more comprehensive than generally supposed. He admitted that moral truth is but a part of literary art:

. . . in the briefest poems of a true thinker we read the essence of the life-long reflections of a passionate and intellectual nature. Fears and hopes common to all thoughtful men have been coined into a single phrase. Even in cases where no definite conviction is expressed or even implied, and the poem is simply, like music, an indefinite utterance of a certain state of the emotions, we may discover an intellectual element. The rational and the emotional nature have such intricate relations that one cannot exist in great richness and force without justifying an inference as to the other. (273)

As Stephen saw it, the greatest poetry reflected the most complex, and at the same time, the most balanced artistic sensibility— the powerful thought and powerful feeling later praised in the twentieth century by the poet T. S. Eliot. Such poetry, to Stephen, is the product of the "richest, most powerful, and most susceptible emotional nature, and the most versatile, penetrative, and subtle intellect," blended to form the "healthiest nature." Disease is "an absence or want of balance of certain faculties" which leads either to faulty reasoning or to an emotional imbalance, both of which he had in mind when he used the term "morbid." Morbidity he related to "immoral," which he at some pains distinguished from "immorality": "An immoral sentiment is the sign either of a false judgment of the world and of human nature, or of a defect in the emotional nature which shows itself by a discord or an indecorum, and leads to a cynicism or indecency which offends the reason through the taste. What is called immorality does not indeed always imply such defects. Sound moral intuitions may be opposed to the narrow code prevalent at the time; or a protest against puritanical or ascetic perversions of the standard may hurry the poet into attacks upon true principles" (274–75). Such passages in Stephen suggest that he felt less subject to the current values of Victorian society as a critic than as an editor.

The imbalance of faculties implicit in his term "morbid" was illustrated for Stephen in the poetry of Shelley and Byron. Stephen praised the "magical verses" of Shelley's "Ode to the West Wind" for their presentation of the "fitful melancholy which oppresses a noble spirit when it has recognized the difficulty of forcing facts into conformity with the ideal." But, while both poets were successful in evoking such moods, neither could deal successfully with the human dilemma which produced the mood. Consequently,

however intense the emotion, and however exquisite its expression, we are left in a state of intellectual and emotional discontent. Such utterances may suit us in youth, when we can afford to play with sorrow. As we grow older we feel a certain emptiness in them. A true man . . . cannot afford to confess himself beaten with the idealist who has discovered that Rome was not built in a day. . . . He has to work as long as he has strength; to work in spite of, even by strength of, sorrow, disappointment, wounded vanity, and blunted sensibilities; and therefore he must search for some profounder solution to the dark riddle of life. (282–83)

And such was to be found in the poetry of Wordsworth who, despite his defects, spoke powerfully to the sorrows of mature existence. Not only accommodation to tragedy but a means of profiting from it are seen in his work.

Stephen appreciated Wordsworth for his general sanity and balance, but he challenged part of his philosophy. As might be expected, his chief objection was to the poet's pantheism which had led the poet to an easy optimism about the universe. For instance, Wordsworth tended to assume that, because of their derivation from nature, human instincts were all good. Stephen reminded his readers that, while some instincts raised man, others obviously degraded him into bestiality. Hence nature's moral teachings are ambiguous unless they are subject to interpretation by the individual's own moral sense.

Admittedly, Wordsworth had a theory about the development of the moral sense through close association with nature in youth. The child's emotions of joy and love, for example, are linked in his memory with the beauty and sublimity of nature. Later, when the world has driven the adult in upon himself, these associations help him to recognize his better, because sounder, impulses. Although Stephen was not entirely convinced that this theory had general application, it was clear to him that it was responsible for one of the poet's artistic strengths: "Nobody has ever shown, with such exquisite power as Wordsworth, how much of the charm of natural objects in later life is due to early associations, thus formed in a mind not yet capable of contemplating its own processes" (290).

Stephen was also impressed by the poet's recognition of the effect of materialism on the individual in the early stages of an industrial society. The tendency of men to regard material acquisitions as ends in themselves produced a diminution of their moral being. A still more pervasive evil, however, was the consequence of the division of labor in an industrial society. In Stephen's words, Wordsworth deplored "the contrast between the old-fashioned peasant who, if he discharged each function clumsily, discharged at least many functions, and found exercise for all the intellectual and moral faculties of his nature, and the modern artisan doomed to the incessant repetition of one petty set of muscular expansions and contractions, and whose soul, if he has one, is therefore rather an encumbrance than otherwise" (297). Rearrangements of the social scheme were irrelevant in the face of this problem. The artist, as did Wordsworth, must give powerful expression to broader views of human nature than men in these circumstances could find for themselves. This particular problem continues in this century, but we can imagine the cynic's inquiry about the numbers of production workers who are at home with Wordsworth's poetry.

Stephen's brand of humanism is best illustrated in the praise which he reserved for the way in which the poet turned adversity to account:

Every element of which our nature is composed may be said to be good in its proper place; and therefore every vicious habit springs out of the misapplication of forces which might be turned to account by judicious training. The waste of sorrow is one of the most lamentable forms of waste. Sorrow too often tends to produce bitterness or effeminacy of character. But it may, if rightly used, serve only to detach us from the lower motives, and give sanctity to the higher. That is what Words- worth sees with unequalled clearness, and he therefore sees also the conditions of profiting. The mind in which the most valuable elements have been systematically strengthened by meditation, by association of deep thought with the most universal presences, by constant sympathy with the joys and sorrows of its fellows, will be prepared to convert sorrow into a medicine instead of a poison. Sorrow is deteriorating so far as it is selfish. The man who is occupied with his own interests makes grief an excuse of effeminate indulgence in self-pity. . . . The man who has learnt habitually to think of himself as part of a greater whole, whose conduct has been habitually directed to noble ends, is purified and strengthened by the spiritual convulsion. His disappoint- ment, or his loss of some beloved objects, makes him more anxious to fix the bases of his happiness widely and deeply, and to be content with the consciousness of honest work, instead of looking for what is called success. (301–2)

Arnold's own estimate of Wordsworth's achievement appeared in 1879 in the preface to an edition of the poet's work which was intended to enhance his reputation through the selection of his best poetry. The preface expressed a desire to save the poet from his admirers, especially those like Stephen who had praised his philosophy. A comparison of the work of the two critics reveals that Stephen's is the more comprehensive treatment. Arnold con- centrated on the joy which the poet found in nature and thus failed to demonstrate the inner strength which this joy stored up against the time when, in the poet's phrase, "the still, sad music of humanity" dominated his sensibility. Perhaps this emphasis was the result of Arnold's desire to stress esthetic rather than philosophic elements. Whatever the explanation, Stephen for once had the advantage over Arnold.

The last *Cornhill* essay which is necessary to a general understanding of Stephen's esthetic views is his "George Eliot," [15] a work often used to illustrate the unsoundness of Stephen's attitude toward fiction. It is true that he began by defending the intrusions of the author into her novels:

We are indeed told dogmatically that a novelist should never indulge in little asides to the reader. Why not? One main advantage of a novel, as it seems to me, is precisely that it leaves room for a freedom in such matters which is incompatible with the requirements, for example, of dramatic writing. I can enjoy Scott's downright storytelling, which never reminds you obtrusively of the presence of the author; but with all respect for Scott, I do not see why his manner should be the sole type and model for all his successors. I like to read about Tom Jones or Colonel Newcome; but I am also very glad when Fielding or Thackeray puts his puppets aside for the moment and talks to me in his own person. (211)

Here, say some critics, is clear evidence of Stephen's distrust of fiction engendered by a Puritan background; for the illusion of reality in fiction is regarded as dishonest. Furthermore, Stephen identified her interpolations as the product of her tendency to reflect upon questions of value, a tendency with which he was naturally sympathetic:

The poor woman was not content simply to write amusing stories. She is convicted upon conclusive evidence of having indulged in ideas; she ventured to speculate upon human life and its meaning, and still worse, she endeavoured to embody her convictions in imaginative shapes, and probably wishes to infect her readers with them. This was, according to some people, highly unbecoming in a woman and very inartistic in a novelist. I confess that, for my part, I am rather glad to find ideas anywhere. They are not very common; and there are a vast number of excellent fictions which these sensitive critics may study without the least danger of a shock to their artistic sensibilities by anything of the kind. (210–11)

The witty irony of this passage reminds us that other novelists with ideas, such as George Meredith and Thomas Hardy, faced a similar difficulty with Victorian critics.

But we must recognize that Stephen was not primarily bent upon the defense of Eliot as a philosophic novelist. On the contrary, he initiated one of the critical views which has continued into the twentieth century: he regarded Eliot as most successful in the early novels. With her powerful memories of nineteenth-century English country life and with the unforgettable characters with which she peopled this world, Eliot was at her best. Up to and including *The Mill on the Floss* (1860), her insights into human psychology blended with her artistic creations. They were for the most part dramatized rather than asserted in asides by the author. Such intrusions, Stephen also felt, were much more seldom found in the body of her work than most critics realized. It is true that Stephen felt that her characters were made memorable both because they were drawn from her memories of rural people and because their creator put them forth as illustrative of the subtle moral dilemmas which appealed to her intellect. In his feeling that Eliot's moral seriousness contributed to her artistic achievement, Stephen anticipated a major development of modern Eliot criticism. F. R. Leavis' *The Great Tradition* (1948) later regarded the maturity and depth of her moral vision as a significant aspect of her artistic achievement.

One of Eliot's special appeals to Stephen in these early novels was her ability to re-create folk humor, for his admiration for this facet of her work was unbounded: "There is something mysterious in the power possessed by a few great humourists of converting themselves for the nonce into that peculiar condition of muddle-headedness dashed with grotesque flashes of common-sense which is natural to a half-educated mind. . . . We require not a new defect of logic, but a new logical structure" (216–17). Such power enriched the sense of life in her novels and hence reinforced the psychological insights which were granted the reader through the lives of her characters.

Again Stephen foreshadowed a tendency of modern Eliot criticism: in this case, the stress on Eliot as an early psychological novelist. In fact, he found the initial development of character more convincing than subsequent plot manipulations. For example, the early years of Maggie Tulliver, the heroine of *The Mill on the Floss,* which saw the flowering of her imagination and intelligence, were highly successful. But, while he admitted that idealistic and sensitive young women were capable of stupidity in love, Maggie's subsequent destructive attachment to the wooden character, Stephen Guest, marred the novel.

After *The Mill on the Floss*, which Stephen regarded as the peak of Eliot's achievement, her intellect began to dominate her imagination, and spontaneity gave way to more calculated effects. The historical novel *Romola* (1863) was, for example, "a magnificent piece of cram. . . . The masses of information have not been fused by a glowing imagination" (228). And, while Stephen felt the strength of *Middlemarch* (1871–72), today generally considered Eliot's masterpiece, he was disturbed by the dominance of her philosophy which made the novel "painful" for him. He also observed that *Middlemarch* exhibited a prosaic quality when set against the idyllic quality of the novels which had preceded it. More disastrous, however, was Eliot's presentation of the novel's heroine, Dorothea Brooke, in whose life Stephen saw an unintentional irony. The novelist had sought to create a high-minded St. Theresa whose passionate devotion to noble aims brought only defeat and tragedy because of the hostility of modern society to all high aspirations. Instead, Dorothea emerged as a shallow, foolish romantic who learned nothing from the reverses she met in life. In Stephen's words, "Had 'Middlemarch' been intended for a cutting satire upon young ladies who wish to learn Latin and Greek when they ought to be nursing babies and supporting hospitals, . . . [the plot] would have been in perfect congruity with the design" (231).

It might be argued that Stephen objected to *Middlemarch* because he found the theme itself unpalatable and was unwilling to admit it, but such an interpretation would ignore the candor of his usual criticism of British society. And his judgment that Eliot's artistic sense was not the equal of her intellect in this novel has been echoed since in the twentieth century.[16] It is clear that Stephen was capable of genuine esthetic insights, however crudely they may be developed by the standards of modern analysis of the technical components of the novel.

Once the broadly humanistic qualities of Stephen's esthetic have been noted, and after it has been seen that he was capable of criticizing some of the more formal aspects of literary art, it must be granted that his criticism reflects a strong biographical interest —one that the Victorian moral esthetic naturally led to. If the reader is to take seriously the content of a novel or a poem, he might logically be expected to concern himself with its creator. At times, Stephen seems to have forgotten the creation in his concern for the character of its creator; we find this quality especially true in a number of his general statements on the topic. Yet the best critical biographies which he contributed to the English Men of Letters series demonstrate that he was fully capable of restricting himself to those aspects of biography directly relevant to the artistic performance of his subject—as is attested to by his *George Eliot* (1902).

Biographical criticism reflects, as we have seen earlier, one of the dominant esthetic concepts of the Victorian period: great art is the product of great men. As Stephen put it in 1877, great art is the product "of a mind fully developed, strengthened by conflict with the world, and enriched by reflection and experience." [17] Four years later he added the statement that the influence of a writer is dependent upon his "total power, upon his intellectual and emotional vigour, upon the strength of his passions, the clearness of his reason, the delicacy of his perceptions, the general harmony of faculties so coordinated and correlated as to give unity and consistency to his whole life and character."

The breadth of Stephen's approach to the character of the artist should not be obscured, however, by his more homely expressions of it. Immediately following the foregoing statement, for instance, he noted a preference, despite many exceptions, for friends met through books, particularly as these influenced his own character. He liked "a man with two or more ideas in his head"; and, if it could be arranged, he would, he said, "like to feel that I might leave him alone in my library or cellar without having afterwards to count my books or my bottles." Like many humanists today, Stephen considered "books as instruments for developing our whole natures." Judicious selection allowed one to "become as intimate as possible with some of the greatest thinkers of mankind" and to assimilate their best ideas.[18]

In Stephen's opinion, biography itself performs an important function for anyone who wishes to understand literature. As he saw it, a sincere and deep appreciation of literature is dependent upon historical criticism which in turn rests upon the history of ideas, social history, and biography.[19] Close textual analysis and the resultant de-emphasis of historical criticism was not to emerge until the twentieth century.

III   Hours in a Library

Composed of thirty-two essays first published in the *Cornhill* from 1868 to 1882, *Hours in a Library,* a three-volume work, might be expected to exhibit the thematic diffuseness often found in books written in this way. Yet the work is solidly cemented both by the consistency of the author's esthetic views and by his point of view which creates a pronounced tonal unity. Stephen's manner is sober and judicious throughout, but it is enlivened by his quiet wit. Whether he is dealing with a personal favorite or a writer whose philosophy is antithetical to his own, Stephen maintains his fairness and independence of judgment. Like J. S. Mill, who saw the strengths of Coleridge and the weaknesses of Bentham despite his own loyalties, Stephen's literary criticism derived intellectual candor from his rationalism.

The spirit of this work is made explicit in the Charlotte Brontë essay. As a critic, Stephen hoped to proceed in a scientific mood "as calmly as if he were ticketing a fossil in a museum." However, while the critic should not shy away from logical analysis, he must first approach his subject with "instinctive sympathy, instead of deliberate reason." Stephen admitted the difficulty of alternating between "witness and judge," but he demonstrated the feasibility of such a position in *Hours in a Library* where his best literary criticism appeared.

The typical essay in this collection is a general estimate of the life and works of an author; in some cases, these essays were later expanded into individual volumes in the English Men of Letters series. Studies of novelists and essayists are much more frequent than those of poets, but the best is the already-discussed essay on Wordsworth. Although there is also somewhat more concentration on nineteenth-century figures than on writers of the previous century, the chosen subjects are those of a critic who is rather more open-minded than the stereotype of the Philistine. It is true that in the first volume (1874), for example, English figures are in the majority; but they are selected from the two centuries preceding his own as well as from the nineteenth century, and two Americans, Jonathan Edwards and Nathaniel Hawthorne, are included as well as a Frenchman, Balzac. Sir Thomas Browne, Daniel Defoe, Samuel Richardson, Alexander Pope, Horace Walpole, Sir Walter Scott, and Thomas De Quincey complete the first volume.

Both witness and judge, Stephen illustrates the ways in which he found these writers personally appealing and then identifies their more universal strengths and weaknesses.

His treatment of Pope is representative. From the time of Byron's defense of Pope against Wordsworth's adverse view early in the nineteenth century, critics have tended to be polarized in their opinions of the two poets. Given the warmth of Stephen's admiration for Wordsworth, we would expect him to be hostile to Pope. Furthermore, such a response would have been in character with that of many Victorian critics who were repelled by recent evidence of Pope's trickery in the publication of his letters; for the poet had arranged for their appearance, then had pretended that they had been published against his wishes. Arnold, who later called Pope no poet at all, dismissed Dryden's and Pope's poetry as classics of English prose in the lead essay of *Essays in Criticism: Second Series* (1888). Stephen is kinder and, at the same time, much closer to twentieth-century views of Pope. While Stephen does not stress Pope's genius for polished and pungent epigrams and while he ignores his variety of mood which is bounded by the Augustan "Rape of the Lock" and the Romantic "Eloisa to Abelard," such deficiencies are typical of Stephen's poetry criticism. On the other hand, his remarks on Pope demonstrate that his esthetic has more utility than generally granted.

Pope's reputation, secure in the twentieth century, is that of an outstandingly successful moral and intellectual poet.[20] While these are the very qualities which would appeal to Stephen, there were two other factors which offset them: one was the poet's life, which was appallingly duplicitous for Victorian readers; the other, the philosophic basis of Pope's poetry—Deism, whose superficial optimism Stephen had already attacked in *English Thought*. But Stephen employs some of his more felicitous phrases to express the amazing survival of Pope's poetry: "In his lifetime 'the wasp of Twickenham' could sting through a sevenfold covering of pride or stupidity. . . . But it is more remarkable that Pope seems to be stinging well into the second century after his death. His writings resemble those fireworks which, after they have fallen to the ground and been apparently quenched, suddenly break out again into sputtering explosions. The waters of a literary revolution have passed over him without putting him out." [21] What surprises Stephen was that Pope's continued success challenged the Victorian assumption that great art was the product of noble artists. The Pope which had just emerged from William J. Courthope's biography in the ten-volume edition (1871–89), edited by Whitwell Elwin, was a proven liar. As Stephen examined his poetry, however, he found that it was demonstrably moral. Here again, Stephen's theories did not destroy his objectivity.

The defects which Stephen noted in Pope were those he saw in the eighteenth century itself, an age of relative simplicity without a sense of the continuity of history. Therefore, when Pope decided to study mankind, he did not "mean man as the product of a long series of generations and part of the universe of inextricably involved forces." He meant, instead, men of his own acquaintance involved in politics and religion which have become, respectively, said Stephen, "a series of petty squabbles for places and pensions, in which bribery is the great moving force," and "a series of bare metaphysical demonstrations too frigid to produce enthusiasm or stimulate the imagination" (I, 98–99). A century of evolution of society beyond its eighteenth-century emergence from a feudal state had naturally produced a more complex analysis of human nature in literature. Consequently, the achievement of clarity in Pope's observations about human nature is nearly canceled by their self-evident quality. "We have the same feeling as when a modern preacher employs twenty minutes in proving that it is wrong to worship idols of wood and stone" (I, 103). For all its truth, Pope's psychology—when measured, say, by Browning's—is elementary.

But, since Stephen was treating Pope as a moralist, the poet's personal character was a more relevant difficulty. Especially reprehensible was the way in which Pope lied and schemed to advance his career. We may gloss this over with the word equivocation; but, as Stephen phrased it, "Pope's equivocation is to the equivocation of ordinary men what a tropical fern is to the standard representatives of the same species in England" (I, 103). But, since Stephen felt that Pope's poetry at its best conveyed a profound moral sense, he was forced to admit the poet exhibited the usual human inconsistency. This recognition left Stephen with the problem of the poet's sincerity. Here he assumed that those lines which stood the test of time were based upon sincere beliefs.

Stephen appreciated Pope's enthusiastic and sincere expressions of contempt for dullness which he found in the *Dunciad*. But he felt that the fortress of dullness was impregnable against the assaults of witty poetry: "It is fighting with a mist, and firing cannon balls into a mudheap. As well rave against the force of gravitation or complain that our gross bodies must be nourished by solid food" (I, 113). Yet such literary sorties against dullness were consistent with Pope's lively and independent wit—and here, therefore, was sincerity.

Observing that Pope was the first English man of letters to achieve financial independence through literature, Stephen asked what moral insights were promulgated from this advantageous position. Pope's morality, not surprisingly, was "the expression of the conclusions of supreme good sense" (I, 118–19). It was clear to Stephen why his contemporaries who were, as he said, "permanently in a passion," would not like or admire Pope. Stephen himself found Pope, both as a critic and as a moralist, "really admirable" (I, 119). For example, no one was more successful in satirizing the literary vices of Neo-Classicism than Pope. He was also among the first to help Shakespeare to his modern reputation.

To judge Pope's general impact as a moralist, Stephen first examined Pope's life, in which he found evidence of a sincere and lasting love for his immediate family and sincere, though elaborate, expressions of friendship for Pope's select circle of friends. Examining the *Essay on Man* (1733–34), he found this benevolence consistent with a certain strain in Pope's poetry. His comments on this work are characteristic, for he observed the extent to which the poet utilized the ideas of his contemporaries such as Shaftesbury, Locke, and Bolingbroke. Some of the contempt of the historian of ideas for those who use other men's ideas is evident: Pope is spoken of as an intellectual parasite.

Stephen also observed the esthetic problem which a poetry of statement presents: he doubted that "the art of reasoning in verse" is "legitimate" (I, 126). He saw the tonal inconsistency which was produced when, for example, religious feeling was juxtaposed with satirical epigrams. Nonetheless, Stephen's experience with the intellectual history of Pope's age let him perceive that the poet's strength derived not only from his polished phrases but from an early poetic intuition of pantheism. It was Pope's pantheism which Stephen found to be the soundest base for the poet's optimism. The Deism of his friends presented inadequacies for poetic use, and Pope at his best showed full awareness of this fact. He then "spoke not of the intelligent moral Governor discovered by philosophical investigation, but of the Divine Essence immanent in all nature, whose 'living raiment' is the world" (I, 131). Although this view is not sustained and is often contradicted, the poet "shows, not merely in set phrases, but in the general colouring of his poem, something of that width of sympathy which should result from the pantheistic view" (I, 131). It is a sympathy which is in the largest sense moral, an outlook epitomized in the couplet: "Never elated, while one man's oppressed;/Never dejected, whilst another's blessed." While Stephen frankly admitted that this was but a partial exposition of Pope's moral vision, he was satisfied of its essential truth.

In the other essays, a similar balance is maintained. A childhood favorite of Stephen's, Sir Walter Scott, was admitted to have his faults. Because of Stephen's admiration for Scott the man, it was all the more difficult to admit that the novelist's secondary characters are more lifelike than his wooden heroes and heroines; that his novels, therefore, break into the many stories of lesser characters; and that his novels are cluttered with historical anachronism. Although Stephen readily granted these deficiencies, he would not accede to Carlyle's complaint that Scott was no prophet. To Stephen, Scott's business was to tell tales, not to prophesy. His strength was to be seen in the spontaneity of his stories, not in their moral message: "Why should not a poet stand aside from the chaos of conflicting opinions . . . and show us what was beautiful in the world as he saw it, without striving to combine the office of prophet with this more congenial occupation?" (I, 147).

Aside from Scott's narrative ability, Stephen praised him for his historical sense as a novelist. Scott's novels are crudely anachronistic, and his settings often partake of the spurious and sham. Despite these qualities, however, his novels revealed a historical sense to Stephen: "To enable us rightly to appreciate our forefathers, to recognize that they were living men, and to feel our close connection with them, is to put a vivid imagination to one of its worthiest uses." Such an artistic achievement is the consequence when "a man whose mind is full of historical associations somehow communicates to us something of the sentiment which they awake in himself" (I, 159–60).

A bare geographical fact or a place name evoked a wealth of

associations for Scott; and this rich historical sense, as Stephen was the first to observe,[22] led the novelist to concrete illustrations of the values of order and tradition to society, values which Edmund Burke had earlier stressed.

The general objectivity of *Hours in a Library* is evident in the treatment of Nathaniel Hawthorne. Assuming the usual twentieth-century view of the moral esthetic, Stephen's own personal commitment to a tragic vision of life should have led him to stress Hawthorne's portrayal of human evil. He chose, instead, to describe the delicate and suggestive quality of the novelist's imagination. Hawthorne's success in fiction was seen as the consequence of his discovery of an answer to the problem of the writer who seeks romantic elements in a pedestrian age. As did Robert Louis Stevenson later, Stephen objected to what he considered the prosaic tendency of the emerging realism.[23] Genuine art required more than this, yet Stephen did not approve of romantic escape. Finally, Hawthorne was one of the few nineteenth-century novelists with whom Stephen felt at home in flights of fancy.

Reared in a prosaic environment, Hawthorne had the kind of imagination which craved a romantic setting with ivy-covered ruins, and Stephen regarded this conflict as the source of the novelist's artistic success. When Hawthorne was forced to seek romantic elements in his drab New England culture, he was at his best. Considered by Victorian critics to be Hawthorne's best work, *The Marble Faun* (1860) demonstrated the undesirable consequences, for Stephen, of finding a romantic setting ready-made for his use. The soundness of choosing transplanted Americans in preference for native Italians was noted. And the creation of Donatello was considered a triumph of Hawthorne's delicate imagination, a character who could only live in a romantic setting. The novel is nevertheless defective as a result of the many guide-book descriptions which are often without any organic relationship to the story. For Stephen, such local color was destructive to the dramatic intensity of the novel, especially at such moments when it becomes more interesting than the story itself.

In Hawthorne's American novels, details of setting formed an inevitable part of the whole. Of these Stephen was most impressed, as many have since been, by the *Scarlet Letter* (1850). The strength of the novel derived from Hawthorne's indirection.

For example, the psychological consequences of Dimmesdale's agreement with Hester to flee New England are shown in his various compulsions to evil behavior with others as he returned from the forest. Any of these contemplated actions would have intensified his already considerable agony; they thus reveal the impact of his desperate decision.

As with many readers since, Hawthorne's suggestiveness, the "fanciful and airy" in his work, became more appealing to Stephen after closer acquaintance. Hawthorne's was a sound tactic for dealing with the historical past of New England, especially his Puritan forefathers whose "old dogmatical framework" had been displaced in Hawthorne's mind by "dreamy speculation, obeying no laws save those imposed by its own sense of artistic propriety" (I, 193). Both the superstitions and values of his ancestors came into his fiction as concrete embodiments of the ancient theology. The appearance of the superstitions was necessary, but they were so muted that they added to the romance rather than offended the reader's taste. The qualities of Hawthorne's fiction which made such subject matter palatable to Stephen were the very qualities most often appreciated by twentieth-century readers—a sense of compassion opposed by a delicate irony.

The writings of Jonathan Edwards presented one of the stiffest challenges to Stephen's objectivity; for, appalled by the Calvinist's dramatization of the doctrine of depravity in his sermons, Stephen was simultaneously attracted by Edwards' place in the history of ideas. The eighteenth-century New Englander, isolated from direct intercourse with the thinkers of his day, managed somehow to become one of America's most original philosophers. His modification of Calvinism anticipated nineteenth-century Transcendentalism; his work also represented the most substantial philosophic thought opposing the eighteenth-century empiricism of Locke and Hume.

Considered by Victorian commentators to be the most successful defender of Calvinism, Edwards was also, for the same observers, disgustingly devoid of a moral sense. The first opinion was based upon his philosophic writings, especially the *Freedom of Will* (1754); the second was the consequence of his sermons, such as *Sinners in the Hands of an Angry God* (1741), which stressed the depravity of all men, even of little children. Stephen admitted the force of both views, but he insisted that closer examination revealed the profoundest moral insight. Readers of the essay "The Nature of True Virtue" in *Two Dissertations* (1765) will recall the distinction Edwards made between benevolent acts based on selfish motives and genuine benevolence, the desire of good for all that exists, a feeling which Edwards derived from his love of God. In his youthful love of God and nature, Edwards had come to believe in their essential identity. Pantheism was the result. Edwards' love of God was then translated into love of the sum of all being, or what he called "benevolence." Such benevolence leads the possessor to seek virtue.

The definition of virtue was broadened by Edwards who conceived of it as moral beauty, the state of being in harmony with all existence. The breadth of such a moral outlook impressed Stephen who found it consistent with the gentle mysticism of Edwards' youth. Elsewhere, too, he admired the depth of the religious views which pervaded the New Englander's life: "Our theory of religion may differ from his; but at least he fully realizes how profound is the meaning of the word, and aims at conquering all human faculties, not at controlling a few external manifestations" (I, 336).

On the other hand, the *Freedom of Will* posed an important difficulty for Stephen. The essay was consistent with the Calvinistic doctrine of unconditional election: some are to be saved; many are not—and the choice is God's. Edwards argued that human will, thought to be free, was subject to universal causation (God); hence it was not free. This view also eliminated chance, which would have made morality meaningless to Edwards. The upshot is a kind of religious determinism which, coupled with "eternal damnation," became quite awful to Stephen as a theological and philosophic position which, combined with eloquence and literary imagination as in *Sinners in the Hands of an Angry God,* produced the most terrible results. In fact, it was representative of the stern theology which had been most influential in Stephen's own agnosticism: man, made weak by God, is thus doomed to fall and to be forever tormented in hell.

Despite his horror of Calvinism, Stephen was objective enough to perceive that Edwards' pantheism had appeared in a sensibility trained in Calvinism. Yet he was troubled by the fact that, as he put it, "amongst some very questionable metaphysics and much outworn—sometimes repulsive—superstition, he grasps the central truths on which all really noble morality must be based."

Stephen dwelt upon Edwards' inconsistency: "he was a kind of Spinoza-Mather; he combines, that is, the logical keenness of the great metaphysician with the puerile superstitions of the New England divine. . . ." (I, 329). Calvinism's doctrines of depravity and unconditional election led to eternal torment for most men, but pantheism led to universal benevolence. As Stephen saw it, the great mind had logic-tight compartments. Twentieth-century students of Edwards are more inclined to argue that love reconciled his system.[24]

The Charlotte Brontë essay most clearly reveals the limits of a rationalistic and moral esthetic. At the same time, an important problem in Stephen's criticism is clarified in it: his often-noticed hostility to the illusion of reality in fiction is less troublesome when more clearly understood. Although twentieth-century critics like David Cecil in his *Early Victorian Novelists* (1935) later regarded Charlotte as the pioneer of the modern psychological novel, Stephen denied her first rank because of the narrowness of her world. And the intensity of Emily's own mystical vision, whose poetic force has so often stirred twentieth-century imaginations, was totally unappreciated by Stephen, who called her *Wuthering Heights* (1857) "a baseless nightmare" (III, 27). Stephen would have been astonished at the praise of Emily's genius by Cecil who was nearly overawed by her vision and her craftsmanship. But the Victorian critic would have been more startled by the twentieth century tendency to rank Emily above Charlotte.

What principally troubled Stephen about Charlotte was the fact that her novels reflected nothing of the turmoil of the Victorian intellectual age, being limited by the author's own secluded life, but he granted that her work revealed the emotional intensity latent in the most ordinary of lives. As he said, her novels at their best are in "a state of the highest electric tension" (III, 9). In his attempt to explain this intensity, Stephen was led to theorize about the type of realism in her fiction. The narrowness of her experience led her to turn in upon herself and to use much of her own life, one which is often almost literally transcribed into her novels.

Stephen criticized this technique in the creation of the character of Paul Emanuel in *Villette* (1853). While Emanuel was her most successful character, Stephen observed that he was too close to the original because of the novelist's adherence to the theory that literature should produce the illusion of reality. For a number of twentieth-century critics, such statements disqualify Stephen as a critic of fiction; but, as he explained himself, it appears that he objected not so much to the illusion of reality as to the novelist's failure to transcend the source of her inspiration. He said, "There is too much of the temporary and accidental—too little of the permanent and essential" (III, 18). This distinction is certainly a valid one: it expresses the difference between the literal truth of a newspaper story and the more universal truth of great fiction. Whether or not we agree that the character Emanuel exhibits this type of artistic deficiency, Stephen surely cannot be faulted for saying that the writer should transform particular experiences into characters with universal qualities.

It is true that the psychological novel of the twentieth century forces the artist to draw upon his own experiences and psychological makeup to greater extent than ever before. Nonetheless, it is evident that the imaginations of the great writers transform the details of their own existence to produce fictional characters which are at once rounded out enough to be convincing yet are universal enough to compel serious attention. For example, while William Golding has doubtless drawn upon some of his own psychological and moral dilemmas to endow the character of Samuel Mountjoy in *Free Fall* (1960) with psychological plausibility, Mountjoy certainly has an independent existence both as an individual and as a type of modern man's search for meaning.

IV   *Stephen as Biographer*

In an era of official biographies which eulogized their subjects, Stephen was instrumental in helping to bring a judicious quality into the genre. The kind of biography he wrote occupies the middle ground between the biographies of his day which produced an image suitable for public tastes and that type of modern biography which reduces archives to reference books stuffed with a welter of facts barely subdued to a recognizable design. Stephen's most successful biographies are soundly grounded on the life and works of his subject. At the same time, an identifiable personal vision of the subject pervades the biography. Uncritical adulation was foreign to his rationalistic temperament. Since his own biographical studies began with eighteenth-century figures, he had been free to exercise greater objectivity than was customary in official biographies of Victorians.

Readers of twentieth-century biographies who are accustomed to psychological analysis in depth will not, of course, find it in Stephen. And sometimes what Stephen calls "psychological" will, for twentieth-century readers, be "moral." But, granting him his own ground rules, how successful was his analysis of the moral quality of those writers he studied? The answer to this question depends upon Stephen's moral vision which, as we have seen, was the basis for his esthetic views. For the agnostic, the meaning of literature, and especially of biography, was to be found in its capacity to perpetuate an ethical sense in society. Literature was to furnish illustrations of the results of a breadth of moral vision and thus enhance the reader's sensitivity to value questions. Religion was to be replaced by literature as a conveyer of ethics.

But what can be said of Stephen's own values? The question is paramount when such values become the principle of selection for the biographer. Stephen's vision of human nature is more broadly humanistic than that modern view which, after Freud, has tended to reduce man to a mere sexual animal; but his ethical sense is not finally sophisticated enough for twentieth-century readers. This crucial matter was thoughtfully analyzed by Professor Annan in his biography, particularly in the chapter entitled "Moral and Immoral Man." Annan felt that Stephen tended to oversimplify character by stressing the distinctions between masculine and feminine traits. To be manly was, most importantly, to subdue one's lusts; to be feminine was to assist such restraint by existing as a model of innocence. More generally, to be manly was to work at those worthwhile pursuits which improve society and to be undaunted by the defeats all men sustain. When a male writer failed to live up to Stephen's idea of the manly, he was called morbid, although this term, too, was often applied to any emotional behavior by a man.

Such emphasis upon conduct generated a more subtle deficiency: Stephen was often blind to the total moral quality of a person which, after all, is composed of good and bad tendencies. The urge to classify a man as bad or good deadens one to the contradictions of human character, and Annan explained this fault of Stephen's by two factors. One was his liberal sensibility, dominated as it was by the rationalistic desire to bring logical order into the chaos of human experience. Such a sensibility is more at home with categories. A more important factor was Stephen's lack of knowledge of human behavior, which was explained by Annan as the consequence of his fear that more knowledge would make moral judgments impossible.

The general truth of Annan's conception of Stephen's moral vision is evident, but, as Stephen's work is considered, it must be qualified. His treatment of Pope, for example, suggests full awareness of the contrary impulses of human nature. And, in the treatment of his esthetic views above, it became clear that Stephen's tastes were broader than they have been generally thought to be. As for the implications of his sexual attitudes, the sexual license which has begun to pervade the Western world in the latter part of our own century indicates that sex is more than a psychological problem. For some, sexual fulfillment has become a kind of ethic of its own, one to be pursued regardless of the consequences for others. Stephen and his age wrongly feared sex, but is it any more sensible to make it a god? Whatever the crudities of Stephen's ethics, however, his own concern with human values was certainly appropriate in view of the fact that his biographies often dealt with figures who regarded themselves as moralists.

Stephen's most important work as a biographer was his editorship of the *Dictionary of National Biography*, which began in 1882. Within two years, individual volumes were appearing quarterly. The labor of the next six years on the huge project took its toll. When Stephen's health began to fail from overwork and he turned the *Dictionary* over to his assistant, Sidney Lee, in 1890, Stephen was responsible for the first twenty-six volumes; Lee prepared the next thirty-seven. The sixty-three volumes contain nearly 30,000 articles from 654 contributors. Stephen himself wrote 378 articles, the research for which would have provided the basis for as many twentieth-century master's theses. His contributions included philosophers and literary men of the seventeenth, eighteenth, and nineteenth centuries. Predictably, Stephen's emphasis was on eighteenth-century figures.

His other biographical work includes the official biographies, *The Life of Henry Fawcett* (1885), his college friend; *The Life of Sir James Fitzjames Stephen* (1895), his brother; the books in the English Men of Letters series, *Samuel Johnson* (1878), *Alexander*

Pope (1880), *Jonathan Swift* (1882), *George Eliot* (1902), and *Hobbes* (1904); and finally, a number of essays which first appeared mainly in the *National Review.* The best of these were later collected in four volumes as *Studies of a Biographer,* which were published in 1898 and in 1902. The life of Fawcett, typical of those which are commemorative in intent, is yet a restrained account which shows its subject as a man of principle active in the vital political issues of the day, the solutions of which tended to broaden democracy. This biography of a popular figure went through five editions in two years.

The pieces collected in *Studies of a Biographer* are more gentle than the earlier *Hours in a Library;* they reveal a greater sensitivity to the emotional qualities of the literary personality being examined. Also, the tendency is more biographical than critical. Of these essays, the twentieth-century reader will probably enjoy most the ones about Ralph Waldo Emerson and Robert Louis Stevenson. The Emerson essay is a remarkably fair estimate of a writer whose temperament was radically different from Stephen's. Emerson emerges as a man who legitimately earned the admiration of his contemporaries through his cosmic optimism.

George Eliot (1902) is the most readable of Stephen's biographical studies. It is an account of her work as a novelist which treats only those events of her life which have a demonstrable relation to her fiction. Roughly chronological in approach, the book is structured by her major works. Stephen's point of view is essentially that of his *Cornhill* essay which we have already discussed: the early Eliot with its vigorous evocation of the rural characters of her Warwickshire youth gave way after *Silas Marner* to fiction made uneven by her increasing thoughtfulness about philosophical and psychological problems. Stephen felt strong admiration for her craftsmanship in the early novels. As might be expected, he was also keenly appreciative of her intellectual courage as she awakened at Coventry from her Evangelical heritage to a full participation in the attacks of Victorian rationalism upon historical Christianity. He dwelt upon her spiritual and intellectual history, one which was made dramatic by a strong religious feeling in conflict with an intellectual rejection of Christian dogma. Out of this dilemma emerged an ever more subtle analysis of the practical consequences of possessing ideals in a world inhospitable to them. The moral problem held great appeal for Stephen, but he recognized that even the soundest ideas are useless unless executed artistically.

The handling of one particular biographical problem, a matter of general concern to Victorians, once again illustrates the moral esthetic in action. The novelist presented conflicting images to her public: her novels made her the great moral teacher; the novelist herself lived with another's husband for many years. Her relationship with George Henry Lewes, which began about 1854, was handled with great objectivity by Stephen: he accepted her position as she herself explained it. Under the circumstances, the arrangement represented the moral equivalent of a legal marriage, a position validated by the pair's conduct during the balance of their lives. At the same time, Stephen recognized an important consequence of the union for the novelist. The famous Sunday afternoon receptions, begun after their move to the Priory in 1863, quickly became audiences for those who wished to pay homage to the genius of Eliot. The affairs were directed by the devoted Lewes whose vivacity saved them from undue solemnity. Yet perhaps they were finally harmful to the artist, for Stephen felt that it was "not altogether healthy for any human being to live in an atmosphere from which every unpleasant draught of chilling or bracing influence is so carefully excluded. Lewes performed the part of the censor who carefully prevents an autocrat from seeing that his flatterers are not the mouthpiece of the whole human race" (145). Eliot herself deliberately avoided reading criticism of her novels, and the insulated quality of the later portion of her life helped to account for those artistic flaws which Stephen saw in her novels.

Eliot's novels were also strongly affected by her intellectual interests. Stephen himself, however, did not condemn her work for didacticism of the usual sort. He observed that critics often lost their objectivity in the face of any didactic intent which they might detect in a work of fiction. He himself did not wish to be preached to with moral platitudes; on the other hand, how could the writer prevent the influence of his reading from being felt in his fiction? Were not his philosophy and his psychology parts of his mental equipment? Stephen felt that they were. When the novelist creates characters to illustrate his conceptual knowledge, he has gone astray; but it is legitimate to create characters from his own experience which also happen to illustrate general human behavior as formalized by philosophy or psychology. Eliot was not at first guilty of building her character from theory. Maggie Tulliver of *The Mill on the Floss* "is profoundly interesting—not because her character has been constructed from psychological formulae, but because when presented it offers problems to the psychologist as fascinating as any direct autobiography." In her early novels such psychology and philosophy as Eliot possessed led the reader to feel "that we are looking through the eyes of a tender, tolerant, and sympathetic observer of the aspirations of muddled and limited intellects" (114–16).

The close relationship of ethics to art which Eliot insisted upon was, predictably, acceptable to Stephen. He was at pains to explain that, in Eliot's case, beauty includes moral beauty, or beauty of character: "The novelist must recognize the charm of a loving nature, of a spirit of self-sacrifice, or of the chivalrous and manly virtues." No moral relativist, Stephen held "that there is some real difference between virtue and vice, and that the novelist will show consciousness of the fact in proportion to the power of his mind and the range of his sympathies" (116–17). But again, as in Stephen's treatment of Jonathan Edwards and Wordsworth, his study of Eliot reveals a broader humanism than moderns are prone to grant the Victorians. A Victorian moralist might logically be expected to praise art which advanced moral causes regardless of its esthetic qualities. Stephen, on the contrary, was critical of the later Eliot novels in which he detected the presence of theories which distorted experience. He preferred the early novels, whose interest stemmed from their fidelity both to rural England and to Eliot's own psychological and intellectual development.

He was most critical of her work in the genre of the historical novel. As a literary historian, he could give her credit for attempting to develop the historical novel. Scott had been successful in creating lively action and memorable characters, but his novels had been blotted with anachronisms. Despite her careful homework, however, Eliot was unable to bring to life the excitement of that Renaissance Florence in which *Romola* (1862–63) was set. An authentic reproduction of the period would have been striking to the Victorian reader: "The combination of artistic inspiration, intellectual audacity, gross superstition, and supreme indifference to morality, gives the shock of entering a new world where all

established formulae break down, or are in a chaotic state of in-
ternecine conflict" (132). When the reader is to move in the society of the Borgias and Machiavelli, he expects to observe a scene
in which "the elementary human passions have been let loose,
when violence and treachery are normal parts of the day's work,
where new intellectual horizons have opened, and yet the old
creeds are still potent, and there is the strangest mingling of high
aspirations and brutal indulgence . . . so . . . that the ruffian is
still religious, and the enlightened reformer fanatically supersti-
tious" (132–33). Unfortunately, such a world does not emerge in
Romola.

The appeal of the novel for Stephen was based upon the appearance of Eliot's typical heroine, for Romola is a high-minded
girl who is denied expression of her ideals because of the ruthless
society in which she found herself. "Romola was, I take it, a
cousin of Maggie Tulliver, though of loftier character, and provided with a thorough classical culture. The religious crisis
through which she had to pass was not due to Savonarola, but to
modern controversies." The actual subject of the book is, then,
"the ordeal through which Romola has to pass, and the tragedy of
a high feminine nature exposed to such doubts and conflicting
impulses as may still present themselves in different shapes"
(136–37). George Eliot's success in the portrayal of such psychological conflicts is an important basis for her reader appeal in the
twentieth century, a fact which verifies Stephen's judgment.

Of all of Eliot's heroines, Maggie Tulliver attracted Stephen
most powerfully. The reason for this was that Maggie transcended
the type. She was given "such reality by the wayward foibles associated with her noble impulses" that her character "glows with a
more tender and poetic charm than any of her other heroines"
(88–89). Dorothea Brooke, the heroine of *Middlemarch,* intended
by her creator to be the most poignant example of the female type
represented by Maggie, failed to attract Stephen's sympathies. As
he had earlier argued in the *Cornhill,* Dorothea's story amounted
to a satire of the young woman whose demands on life are impractical. Stephen also sensed that Eliot's attitude was not entirely
ironic. Both compassion and irony were evident to him in the
handling of Dorothea's life. Nonetheless, he was more attracted to
Lydgate and to the story of his defeat, a character whose energies
and ambitions were thwarted by the limits of his shallow wife

Rosamund. Despite Eliot's failure to carry out her intentions, accomplishments of this order compelled Stephen to acknowledge her great achievement as a novelist in *Middlemarch.*

Stephen's characteristic independence appears in his judgment of the multiple-plot structure of *Middlemarch.* One of the most surprising features of Victorian criticism is the conscious adherence to the theory of structural unity, a theory which had emerged as early as 1868.[25] Critics urged organic unity upon the diffuse Victorian novel, which were often structured by the stories of many characters. The four-element plot of *Middlemarch* was, in Stephen's opinion, admirably suited to the creation of a realistic portrayal of human relations in English provincial society. His judgment, then, represents a challenge of a fashionable theory, a challenge whose validity has been confirmed by twentieth-century studies of the novel.

Twentieth-century scholarship on *Middlemarch,* as well as the whole modern critical approach to fiction, informs a recent commentary on the novel by David Daiches. Yet he agrees that the Prelude which introduces the St. Theresa theme is misleading. The Prelude establishes the characteristic ambiguity of tone: compassion and irony. Yet the novel is not Dorothea's, for her story is seen as a successful means of drawing the reader into the larger story, which is "the author's mature vision of the mutual interaction between different lives in a given society." [26] Thus, while the twentieth-century student of Eliot may, for instance, smile to himself about Stephen's fondness for Maggie, he must finally admit the validity of many of Stephen's initial judgments of the novelist's work.

V   English Literature and Society in the Eighteenth Century

Published in 1904, the year of Stephen's death, *English Literature and Society* still holds worth for the general reader. It is the culmination of half a century of thought about the period of English literature which it treats. Written as a lecture to give an Oxford audience an overview of the vast topic, the book is less a formal lecture than a literary conversation. It is marked by occasional indirection, by lucid exposition of key intellectual concepts, by a sure grasp of the social and political history as then known, and by deft estimates of prominent literary figures. One of the more successful attempts of Victorian critics to approach literary history through sociology, it was a marked advance over the rigid determinism of Hippolyte Taine (1828–93), the French historian and critic whose *History of English Literature* had been translated into the English in 1873.

Taine's work, in Stephen's opinion, was important because of its attempt to employ a genuine comparative method, but it was finally deficient because of its primitive sociology. Taine's history was based upon crudely inadequate assumptions about the British national character; but, to some extent, the same general criticism might be leveled against Stephen's own work. However, considering Marxist criticism which later appeared in the twentieth century, Stephen's work is far more subtle. For example, while he declined to discuss the nature of literary genius, he admitted that it was an important consideration which was beyond historical or sociological explanations. Marxist criticism, on the other hand, was rigidly deterministic: the individual artist's role was nil.

Confusion of purpose has been seen in *English Literature and Society*. Is it a study of literature to reveal the history of ideas, or a study of the social and political backgrounds of literature for its better understanding? [27] This question is more valid in the case of the earlier *English Thought*, for in it Stephen's emphasis was clearly that of the historian of ideas. In *English Literature and Society*, he put his emphasis upon literature as the by-product of society.

It is true that *English Literature and Society* opens with a discussion of the use of literature for the historian of ideas: literature, that is, is first seen as an expression of the prevailing ideas of a period. But Stephen's purpose in speaking of the problems of the historian of ideas was to introduce an analogous development in literary history. The literary historian who had once judged writers by their adherence to Classical concepts of great literary art can now take the historical approach which qualifies absolute judgments with observations about the fitness of a work of art to its own age: "We can then become catholic enough to appreciate varying forms; and recognize that each has its own rules, right under certain conditions. . . ." [28] Great literature epitomizes universal human truths, yet these truths are expressed in the concrete terms most appropriate to the age in which it appears. The social, political, and philosophic contexts are then indispensable for full appreciation of a great artist, for the critic must distinguish between the qualities due to the artist's genius and those derived from his era.

Generally, Stephen described literary change in the eighteenth century as the consequence of changing intellectual, social, and political attitudes among readers and of an expanding middle class. The displacement of court politics by parliamentary politics with the attendant consequences for literary patronage; the rise of the middle class as a result of political and economic developments and the effect of this upon prose style and the development of the novel; and the decline of the theater as a function of the tastes of an emerging class—these are Stephen's topics. Set against the earlier *English Thought,* this work reflects greater sensitivity to one of the most important esthetic problems of the age: the various meanings of the word "nature." Stephen differentiates among the several nature concepts of Pope and Addison, Richardson and Fielding, Rousseau, Scott, and Wordsworth, thus preparing the way for the more elaborate analysis soon to follow. Furthermore, the industrial revolution is recognized, as it was not in the earlier work, as the source of social problems which would later require reform and also as a factor in the spread of literary culture from its London center. Wealth and leisure from manufacturing made possible the development of such towns as Manchester, Birmingham, and Edinburgh as locations for intellectual activity.

The application of Stephen's method to eighteenth-century literary history led him to his theory of the emergence of great literature: it comes when the individual genius appears who is in complete accord with his society. It "must be produced by the class which embodies the really vital and powerful currents of thought which are moulding society. The great author must have a people behind him; utter what he really thinks and feels and what is thought and felt most profoundly by his contemporaries" (129). The success of Robert Burns illustrated Stephen's theory: "lyrical poetry seemed to have died out in England. It suddenly comes to life in Scotland and reaches unsurpassable excellence within certain limits, because a man of true genius rises to utter the emotions of a people in their most natural form without bothering about canons of literary criticism" (129).

It is true that Stephen's theory would not entirely explain the twentieth-century fame of those writers from Thomas Hardy to

James Joyce and of others of this century whose values are often at odds with their society. As we have seen, Stephen's literary experiences had often presented him with the picture of the artist at one with his audience as entertainer and teacher. But he was surely aware of the ways in which the Romantic poets, the Victorian prophets such as Carlyle, Mill, and Arnold, and even the novelists like George Eliot and Thomas Hardy found themselves critical of nineteenth-century public values. Stephen himself had first taken the role of social critic, and a clue is to be seen in his attitude toward this role: he saw the social critic as far less important than the artist whose writing embodies a worthy and unique vision of human nature. The great writer, then, both speaks for his age and, at the same time, transcends it.

The literary history of the eighteenth century Stephen presented is a distinct development beyond his earlier account in *English Thought*. But the same general statements made earlier about this work are still applicable to *English Literature and Society*. Half a century of subsequent scholarship has naturally refined our concepts of this period. The result has been a number of special studies which have filled in Stephen's outline of a huge topic. Yet, like other of his works, *English Literature and Society* is still in print—a testimony to the fact that it can still provide the general reader with a sound introduction.

VI *Conclusion*

The rationalism of Stephen's Cambridge days which led him to his success as a historian of ideas also operated to qualify his achievement in that discipline, and Stephen's career as a literary critic shows the same mixed bag. Where rationalistic criticism was appropriate to correct nineteenth-century excesses of intuition and emotion, his criticism was most effective. But, where emotion was more important as in poetry, Stephen's tendency to deny the validity of experience outside the rationalistic sphere reduced this achievement. To express it another way, like other Victorian rationalists, Stephen was his most extreme when he encountered philosophical idealism or religion, his most humane when he wrote about literature.

Once the desiccating effect of rationalism in Stephen's writing is understood, the balancing effect of those more physical activities in Stephen's life such as his alpine experiences should also be admitted. These experiences produced *The Playground of Europe,* a work outstanding in the genre of British travel literature. The harmful effects of his rationalism were further mitigated by his work as a biographer. For the twentieth-century reader his biographies lack psychological depth, but fairness here demands recognition of the fact that in comparison with official Victorian biographies his give evidence of much greater candor.

Stephen's record is also distinguished by his accomplishments in important editorial posts but, perhaps most of all, by his pioneering work in the history of ideas. However, when the pendulum of criticism completes its swing away from the practices of the New Critics, Stephen's solid achievement as a literary critic will surely locate him in the company of Matthew Arnold. This is especially true of his contributions to studies of the eighteenth century and of the novel. After all, Stephen began his own criticism of the novel almost two decades before Henry James was prepared to argue that the novel was a serious form of art. However "unesthetic" Stephen's criticism may seem to some twentieth-century critics, the validity of a number of his important judgments about literary figures of the eighteenth and nineteenth centuries must be granted.

Notes and References

Chapter One

1. See Noel G. Annan's excellent Chapter III on Evangelicalism in his *Leslie Stephen* (Cambridge, Mass., 1952).
2. Annan, p. 118.
3. Frederic W. Maitland, *The Life and Letters of Leslie Stephen* (New York and London, 1906), p. 28, hereafter cited in the text as *Maitland*.
4. "Thoughts of an Outsider: The Public Schools," *Cornhill*, XXVII (Mar., 1873), 290.
5. Annan, pp. 28–29.
6. "Some Early Impressions," *National Review*, XLII (1903), 141–42. Subsequent page references are to this volume. This was a four-part series which ran from September through December.
7. For Stephen's own recollections of the problems of university life, particularly the tendency of the institution to "subordinate education or the promotion of intellectual activity to the interests of" the colleges, see "Some Early Impressions," 133–39.
8. *Ibid.*, pp. 138–39.
9. My use of the term "rationalism" differs in no way from the usual understanding of the term among students of the Victorian period, but a definition may be helpful to the general reader. In the eighteenth century, the term "rationalism" commonly described a method of defending religious belief. Human reason was used to explain supernatural happenings. At the same time, thinkers, such as Voltaire and Hume, began to employ reason against religion. I recognize that Hume is generally considered an empirical philosopher in contrast with the continental rationalists from Descartes on. Yet in essence, Hume's attack upon religion is basically rationalistic. Beginning with the nineteenth century, rationalism is commonly used to denote the use of reason to attack religion in the writings of Bentham and the Mills. Rationalism in this sense does not mean rationality, which is generally taken to suggest the general employment of reason in human affairs.
10. *Life of Henry Fawcett* (London, 1885), pp. 23, 37–38.

11. *The English Utilitarians* (New York, 1950), III, 76.

12. "Some Early Impressions," p. 216.

13. Herbert Spencer, in his recollections of the appearance of Mill's *Logic,* speaks of the natural sciences as limited to collecting and collating facts. See the *Autobiography* (London, 1904), II, 247.

14. Mill's objection to the inductive procedure would not have been troublesome to modern historians of the philosophy of science who feel that a more descriptive statement of the scientific method would note the movement from hypothesis to inductive verification.

15. Spencer, pp. 247–48.

16. "Some Early Impressions," p. 146.

17. *Ibid.*

18. *Studies of a Biographer* (New York, 1907), III, 250–51.

19. Claire-Elaine Engel, *A History of Mountaineering in the Alps* (London, 1950), p. 124.

20. "Leslie Stephen," *My Alpine Jubilee, 1851–1907* (London, 1908), p. 87.

21. The first volume of this collection of essays by the members of the Alpine Club appeared in 1859; the second and third, in 1862. The successful sales of these works (the first volume went through five editions in a year) led to the publication of the first volume of *The Alpine Journal* in 1863.

22. Charles R. Darwin, *Autobiography* (London, 1958), pp. 138–39.

23. Lyell, *Principles of Geology* (London, 1830), I, 75.

24. "Some Early Impressions," p. 214.

25. Annan, pp. 162–66.

26. Stephen recapitulated the English attitude this way: "that both sides are such a set of snobs and blackguards that we only wish they could both be licked, or that their armies are the scum of the earth and the war got up by contractors, or that the race is altogether degenerate and demoralized, and it is pleasant to see such a set of bullies have a fall" (Maitland, 122).

27. *Holmes-Einstein Letters,* ed. James Bishop Peabody (New York, 1964), p. 14.

28. A series of Stephen's letters during this period, not, I believe, published elsewhere, are found in the unpublished doctoral dissertation by Samuel Sillen, "Leslie Stephen: A Study in Critical Theory" (University of Wisconsin, 1935). This was the first full-length study of Stephen in the twentieth century.

29. *Letters of Charles Eliot Norton,* eds. Sara Norton and M. A. De Wolfe Howe (London, 1913), II, 267.

Chapter Two

1. "Early Impressions," p. 421. Macaulay and Thackeray had died before Stephen reached London. In 1865, these works, among others, appeared: Carlyle's *Frederick the Great* (final volume), Dickens' *Our Mutual Friend* (serialization concluded in this year), Swinburne's *Atalanta in Calydon*, Arnold's *Essays in Criticism* (first series), Mill's *Sir William Hamilton*, Ruskin's *Sesame and Lilies*, Carrol's *Alice in Wonderland*, and Trollope's *Belton Estate* (serial publication).

2. By 1882 W. F. Poole could say in the preface to his famous *Index to Periodical Literature*, "The best writers and the great statesmen of the world, where they formerly wrote a book or pamphlet, now contribute an article to a leading review or magazine, and it is read before the month is ended in every country in Europe. . . . Every question finds its latest and freshest interpretation in the current periodicals."

3. "Early Impressions," p. 422.

4. The moralistic basis of the judgments of some modern liberals is more cleverly disguised. In Lionel Trilling's introduction to the Viking *Portable Matthew Arnold*, (New York, 1949), he suggests that any position which is not liberal is nonintellectual (433).

5. "Early Impressions," pp. 424, 426. Public opinion means, in this case, middle-class opinion, except in the case of the *Times*, which represented upper-class opinion for the most part.

6. *Ibid.*, p. 431.

7. *Ibid.*, p. 433.

8. "An American Protectionist," VII (1862), 126–32.

9. "The Good Old Cause," *Nineteenth Century*, LI (1902), 11–23.

10. *Cornhill*, XIII (1866), 28–43.

11. Arnold's "The Function of Criticism at the Present Time," had appeared in the *National Review* (1864). Here he had attacked English criticism for its lack of "disinterestedness" which causes it to support the middle-class tendencies toward smugness and self-satisfaction (what Arnold meant by "Philistinism").

12. "Richardson's Novels," *Cornhill*, XVII (1868), 48–69, and "Defoe's Novels," *Cornhill*, XVII (1868), 293–316. Both appear in the first series of *Hours in a Library* (1874).

13. "Richardson's Novels," *ibid.*, p. 52.

14. *Ibid.*, p. 54.

15. See, for example, Ian Watt's *The Rise of the Novel* (Berkeley and Los Angeles, 1962).

16. *Cornhill*, XIX (1869), 575–82.

17. "The Function of Criticism at the Present Time," *op. cit.* In this essay Arnold had expanded the province of the literary critic to include the obligation of social criticism.

18. The publication of Carlyle's *Sartor Resartus* had met with universal disapproval from subscribers, some of whom came to Fraser's office to curse the piece. See David Alec Wilson, *Carlyle to "The French Revolution"; 1826–1837* (New York and London, 1924), p. 362.

19. "The Comtist Utopia," *Fraser's Magazine*, LXXX (1869), 1–21.

20. "Ritualism," *Macmillan's Magazine*, XVII (1868), 479–94.

21. "Dr. Pusey and Dr. Temple," *Fraser's Magazine*, LXXX (1869), 722–37.

22. "The Broad Church," *Fraser's Magazine*, LXXXI (1870), 311–25. This was to be the lead essay of his *Freethinking and Plainspeaking* (1873), a collection of his rationalistic essays from *Fraser's* and the *Fortnightly Review* which defines his agnosticism.

23. *Fraser's Magazine*, LXXXV (1872), 409–21. Darwin's *The Descent of Man* had applied his theory to the "human animal" the year before.

24. *Fraser's Magazine*, LXXXVI (1872), 545–61.

25. See, for instance, Viktor E. Frankl's own empirical observations about what gave his life meaning as he faced death in a Nazi concentration camp during World War II in his *Man's Search for Meaning* (New York, 1963).

26. In *The Nineteenth Century: A Review of Progress* (New York: 1901).

27. Much of Meredith's fiction after *Richard Feverel* (1859) first appeared in the *Fortnightly*.

28. See Edwin M. Everett, *The Party of Humanity: "The Fortnightly Review" and Its Contributors, 1865–1874* (Chapel Hill, 1939), for a full account of the magazine's relation to Victorian thought. See also the pioneer historian of ideas, J. B. Bury, *The Idea of Progress* (New York, 1955), pp. 163–64.

29. John Morley, *Critical Miscellanies* (London, 1923), pp. 74–75.

30. Alan Brown, *Metaphysical Society: Victorian Minds in Crisis, 1869–1880* (New York, 1947), pp. 224–27.

31. Lionel Trilling, *The Liberal Imagination* (Garden City, N.Y., 1953). Trilling has reference to the twentieth-century liberal tendency to simplify and qualify emotions and ideas, to try to fit them into both rationalistic preconceptions and bureaucratic organizations. The phenomenon is equally evident in nineteenth-century liberalism from the Utilitarians on. Stephen himself criticized J. S. Mill's dogmatic liberalism in "An Attempted Philosophy of History," *Fortnightly Review*, XXXIII (May, 1880), 672–95, and by 1902 anticipated Trilling's position as he critiqued the liberalism of his youth (See above in this chapter).

32. "The Age of Reason," *Fortnightly Review,* n.s., XXI (1877), 357, 359.

33. Bury, *Progress, passim.*

34. *Fortnightly Review,* XXXIII (1880), 679–80.

35. *Ibid.,* New Series, V (1869), 129–45.

36. When their ideas are compared with those of one of the most thoroughgoing materialists of the nineteenth century, Louis Büchner, the German physician, it is evident that they were limited materialists. Büchner's *Force and Matter: Empirico-Philosophical Studies, Intelligibly Rendered* (1855), which saw fifteen editions by 1884, was the materialist's bible.

37. William James, *Pragmatism: A New Name for Some Old Ways of Thinking* (New York, London, and Toronto; 1959), p. 51. James had applied the pragmatic method of the American philosopher C. S. Peirce (1839–1914) to religious matters. See also James's *Varieties of Religious Experience* (1902) for his application of the method.

38. Translated from Einstein's *The World as I See It* (1929) by Leopold Infeld in his *Albert Einstein: His Work and Its Influence on Our World* (London and New York, 1950), pp. 116–17.

39. See Brown's *The Metaphysical Society* (New York, 1947) for a full account of the membership and discussions of the group.

40. *Collected Essays* (New York, 1902) V, 245–46.

41. Annan, p. 171.

42. Cyril Bibby, *T. H. Huxley: Scientist, Humanist and Educator* (London, 1959), p. 60. Bibby's book is readable and generally judicious; his warmth of feeling for Huxley causes him to exhibit a mild concern whenever Huxley reveals any sign of a "conservative prejudice."

43. *An Agnostic's Apology* (London, 1903), pp. 1–2. Hereafter cited as *Apology.*

44. The first chapter appeared as "An Agnostic's Apology," *Fortnightly Review,* XXV (1876), 840–60. Four of the seven chapters appeared in the *Fortnightly* between 1876 and 1878.

45. See A. O. Lovejoy, *The Great Chain of Being* (New York, 1960).

46. *Autobiography* (London, 1958), pp. 90, 88.

47. *Ibid.,* pp. 366–67. These selections are from the last chapter which had first appeared in the *North American Review* as "The Religion of All Sensible Men," CXXX (1880), 438–61.

48. Kingsbury Badger, "Christianity and Victorian Religious Confessions," *Modern Language Quarterly,* XXV (1964), 86–109.

49. Annan, pp. 191, 93.

50. A convenient approach to ascertaining the elements of this crucial modern dilemma may be found by reading Joseph Wood Krutch's

The Modern Temper (1929) and *The Measure of Man* (1954). Reconsidering the position of his earlier work in the latter, he makes an interesting case for a limited freedom of will for man.

51. For some other reasons to account for the phenomenon of mountaineering, see Ronald Clark, *The Victorian Mountaineers* (London, 1953), and also chapters 2 and 3 of my unpublished doctoral dissertation, "The Beauty of the Alps: A Study of the Victorian Mountain Aesthetic" (University of Colorado, 1962).

52. F. W. Hirst (ed.), *Early Life and Letters of John Morley* (London, 1927), I, 228.

53. One of the reasons for the excellence of the *Playground* is found in the fact that, like many Victorian books, it was assembled from previously published essays which had appeared in the Alpine Club's *Peaks, Passes and Glaciers* (second series), the *Alpine Journal*, the *Cornhill Magazine*, and *Fraser's Magazine*.

54. *Playground* (Oxford, 1936), p. 240.

55. *Ibid.*, pp. 181–82.

56. *Ibid.*, p. 182.

57. The seventeenth-century origins of the concept of the sublime are developed in Marjorie Nicolson's *Mountain Gloom and Mountain Glory* (Ithaca, N.Y., 1959). See also my unpublished doctoral dissertation, *op. cit.*, for further treatment of the idea during the nineteenth century.

58. *Playground*, pp. 180–81.

59. *Ibid.* (London, 1871), pp. 48–49.

60. *Ibid.* (1936 ed.), pp. 18–19.

61. *Ibid.* (1871 ed.), pp. 65–66.

62. *Ibid.* (1936 ed.), pp. 218–19.

63. *Ibid.*, p. 142.

64. *Ibid.*, pp. 198–99.

65. *Ibid.*, pp. 190–91.

66. See Wordsworth's letter to the *Morning Post* (Dec. 9, 1844) in *The Poetical Works*, ed. William Knight, VII (Edinburgh, 1886), 301–11.

67. *Modern Painters*, III, 198–99, Vol. V, in *The Works of John Ruskin*, ed. E. T. Cook and Alexander Wedderburn (London and New York), pp. 301–12.

68. *Playground* (1871 ed.), p. 27.

Chapter Three

1. C. E. Norton (ed.), *Letters of James Russell Lowell* (New York, 1893), II, 184.

2. *Life of Henry Fawcett* (London, 1885), p. 81.

3. See Oscar Maurer, "Leslie Stephen and the *Cornhill Magazine*,

1871–82," *Studies in English* (Univ. of Texas), XXXII (1953), 67–95, for a readable and judicious account of Stephen's editorship. Maurer finds Stephen's experience with the *Cornhill* illustrative of the "Victorian dilemma" since his brilliance as editor which produced its high literary quality could not achieve financial success (67). Maurer's account emphasizes the effect of the declining popularity of the literary essay on circulation. Earlier, Brown in *Metaphysical Society*, p. 221, had cited the decline of the serial novel as a causal factor.

4. Stephen's *Hours in a Library* (1874, 1876, 1879); Stevenson's *Virginibus Puerisque* (1881) and *Familiar Studies of Men and Books* (1882); Gosse's *Seventeenth-Century Studies* (1883); and Symonds' *Sketches in Italy and Greece* (1874).

5. "Early Impressions," p. 565.

6. Maurer, *op. cit.*, pp. 82, 84–85.

7. Annan, p. 67. Twenty-first century critics will probably conclude that the nineteenth century was undersexed and that the twentieth century was oversexed.

8. Maurer, *op. cit.*, pp. 87–88. In his dealings with the manuscripts of Thomas Hardy, Stephen himself regretted the prudish approach which he felt necessary for the *Cornhill* audience.

9. William R. Rutland, *Thomas Hardy: A Study of His Writings and Their Background* (New York, 1962), p. 79.

10. See Florence Emily Hardy's *The Early Life of Thomas Hardy, 1840–1891* (London, 1928), pp. 132, 167, and also her *The Later Years of Thomas Hardy, 1892–1928* (New York, 1930), p. 88. Rutland (*op. cit.*, pp. 79–80) notes the influence of Stephen's rationalism most in *Tess*.

11. *The Novels and Tales of Henry James* (New York, 1909), XVIII, v–vi.

12. John Connell, *W. E. Henley* (London, 1949), 65–68. The poem appeared in the *Cornhill* in July, 1875.

13. Maitland, p. 353–54.

14. Alfred North Whitehead, *Adventures of Ideas* (New York, 1952), p. vii.

15. See Brown, *The Metaphysical Society*, p. 223. According to Brown, Stephen dissipated his energies because of the many markets open to him for essays.

16. *English Thought in The Eighteenth Century* (New York, 1962) I, 320, hereafter cited above in the text as *Thought*. See also Stephen's essay, "An Attempted Philosophy of History," *Fortnightly*, n.s., XXVII (1880), 672–95. Here, besides his Social Darwinism, Stephen also explicitly rejects Buckle's rationalistic view of history. Buckle had acquired his rationalism from J. S. Mill, the inheritor of the English empirical tradition which Hume had inaugurated. And, as Stephen saw

it, Mill had demonstrated an "incapacity to appreciate adequately the importance of any theory of evolution" (p. 672). Stephen felt that an evolutionary theory would have allowed the empiricists to annex history. As it was, Buckle's history still represented to Stephen the "first and only considerable attempt to construct a science of history upon the basis of English empiricism" (p. 680).

17. In *Three Essays on Religion* (New York, 1874), p. 126.

18. John W. Bicknell, "Leslie Stephen's 'English Thought in the Eighteenth Century': A Tract for the Times" *Victorian Studies*, VI (1962), 103–20. Professor Bicknell's judicious unpublished doctoral dissertation, "Leslie Stephen as Intellectual Historian" (Cornell University, 1950), represents the fullest account of the strengths and weaknesses of *English Thought*.

19. In Stephen's review of Taine's *History of English Literature* in *Fortnightly*, XX (Dec., 1873), 693–714, he praised Taine for employing a comparative approach which included a description of the literature in light of its connection with environment. He noted, however, that the method was limited by an inadequate knowledge of human nature, especially as regards the impact of environment. He said, "Trying to describe the peculiarities of a race or climate, we feel at once the absence of anything like a scientific nomenclature. . . . Far from having arrived at a state of prediction, we have not arrived at a state of trustworthy observation" (694). These statements also help to account for Stephen's failure to follow a more sociological approach.

20. F. W. Bateson, "God-Killer," *New Statesman*, LXV (1963), 945–46.

21. Objections began with J. M. Robertson's *History of Free Thought* (London, 1936, 4th ed.), who supported the Deists over the Orthodox. Both Norman Torrey, *Voltaire and the English Deists* (New Haven, Conn., 1930), and Ernest C. Mossner, *Bishop Butler and the Age of Reason* (New York, 1936), later agreed that Stephen had mistaken the historical importance of the Deists. Despite this fact, we must agree with A. W. Benn, *The History of English Rationalism in the Nineteenth Century* (New York, 1962), who, in the 1906 edition of this work, labeled Stephen's account a "partial vindication of their services" (II, 387).

22. See Mossner, *Bishop Butler*, pp. 18 ff. for details of this censorship.

23. Bicknell, *op. cit.*, p. 205.

24. "Age of Reason," *Fortnightly*, XXVII (Mar., 1877), 356.

25. One readable and judicial account of these matters which includes their relevance to literature is Basil Willey's *The Seventeenth Century Background* (New York, 1953). A more purely philosophic account can be found in chapters 21–23 of W. T. Jones's *A History of*

Western Philosophy (New York, 1952). See also Marjorie Nicolson's *Mountain Gloom and Mountain Glory*, which, while treating a particular problem in esthetic history, details the impact of the new astronomy as well as theories of the earth's age upon English religion and literature.

26. The general reader interested in this matter might begin with Basil Willey's "David Hume," Chapter VII of his *The Eighteenth Century Background* (Boston, 1961), especially pp. 126–35. See also C. W. Hendel, *Studies in the Philosophy of David Hume* (Princeton, N.J., 1925), and Norman Kemp Smith, *The Philosophy of David Hume* (London, 1941).

27. Stephen mentions Lord Herbert of Cherbury (1583–1648) elsewhere in *English Thought* (I, 163) as the pioneer of Deism.

28. Stephen merely noted the general threat to the orthodox idea of the earth's age. The sequence of literary and scientific events was later identified by Marjoric Nicolson in her *Mountain Gloom and Mountain Glory*.

29. For another view of Woolston, see A. W. Benn, *The History of English Rationalism in the Nineteenth Century*, I, 129–34. For the intransigent rationalist Benn, Woolston was a martyr to freethinking.

30. See Basil Willey's chapter on Butler in his *The Eighteenth Century Background*. For another view, see Benn, *op. cit.*, I, 138–45.

31. Willey, *Eighteenth Century Background*, p. 111.

32. See Jerome B. Schneewind, "Moral Problems and Moral Philosophy in the Victorian Period," *Victorian Studies*, Supplement to Vol. IX (Sept., 1965), pp. 29–46.

33. This problem in ethics is another of those matters which receives a more balanced treatment in Willey's *Eighteenth Century Background* (see p. 92).

34. "Dr. Whewell on Moral Philosophy," *Westminister Review* (Oct., 1852).

35. See Willey's *Eighteenth Century Background* for an equally sympathetic but also broader view of Burke's contribution to English thought.

36. The word appears in Stephen's summary, but Paine's doctrines are spoken of as merely the opposite of Burke's. Matthew Arnold had earlier noted Burke's services to an "epoch of concentration" as distinct from the services necessary in an "epoch of expansion" such as the Victorian period. ("The Function of Criticism at the Present Time," *Essays in Criticism* [1869].)

37. Benn, *History of English Rationalism*, I, 216–18.

38. See my unpublished dissertation, "The Beauty of the Alps: A Study of the Victorian Mountain Aesthetic." Mountain poetry equal to the work of the Romantics seldom appears among the Victorians be-

cause they lacked a world view appropriate to a single-minded exaltation of alpine scenery.

39. See Kenneth Graham's *English Criticism of the Novel; 1865–1900* (London, 1965) for full details of Victorian theories of the novel. See also Ian Watt's *The Rise of the Novel* (London, 1957) for the social matrix of the eighteenth-century novel and its effect upon the genre.

40. *The Science of Ethics* (New York, 1882), p. 33. Subsequent citations are identified by page numbers in the text.

Chapter Four

1. Morley, *Recollections* (New York, 1917), I, 117.

2. See Buckley's chapter "The Moral Aesthetic," in his *The Victorian Temper* (Cambridge, Mass., 1951); see also p. 10. An excellent summary of the poetic manifestations of the esthetic is to be found in Alba H. Warren's *English Poetic Theory, 1825–1865* (Princeton, N.J., 1950).

3. Morley, I, 119.

4. The affirmative side is best represented by Annan, pp. 255–56; the negative receives succinct exposition in René Wellek's *History of Modern Criticism: 1750–1950; Vol. IV, The Later Nineteenth Century* (New Haven and London, 1965), 185.

5. "Matthew Arnold," *Studies of a Biographer*, Vol. I. (New York and London, 1898), pp. 81–82.

6. MacCarthy's position appeared in his Leslie Stephen lecture at Cambridge in 1937. W. D. Leavis responded in an essay, "Leslie Stephen: Cambridge Critic," *Scrutiny*, VII (Mar., 1939), pp. 404–15.

7. Wellek, *A History of Modern Criticism: 1750–1950; Vol. IV, The Later Nineteenth Century*, pp. 185–90, 223.

8. *Cornhill*, XXXIV (Nov., 1876), 556–69.

9. "The Moral Element in Literature," *Cornhill*, XLIII, 50.

10. Discussed in Chapter 2.

11. "The Late Lord Lytton as Novelist," *Cornhill*, XXVII (1873), 345–54.

12. *Cornhill*, XXXII, 91–101.

13. *Cornhill*, XXXIV, 206–26, reprinted in *Hours in a Library*, II. Citations in the text are from the 1892 edition.

14. "Wordsworth's Ethics" continues to be included among the best introductory critical accounts of Wordsworth. See Ernest Bernbaum, *Guide through the Romantic Movement* (New York, 1949), p. 104.

15. *Cornhill*, XLIII (1881), 152–68, reprinted in *Hours in a Library*, III. Citations in the text are from the 1892 edition.

16. See, for example, David Cecil, *The Early Victorian Novelists* (London, 1934).

17. "Genius and Vanity," *Cornhill,* XXXV (June, 1877), 684.

18. "The Moral Element in Literature," *Cornhill,* XLIII (Jan., 1881), 41.

19. "The Study of English Literature," *Cornhill,* LV (May, 1887), 492–99.

20. George Sherburn, *The Restoration and Eighteenth Century* (1660–1789), Vol. III; *A Literary History of England* (New York, 1948), pp. 921–32.

21. *Hours in a Library* (London, 1892), I, 94. Subsequent citations from this edition are identified in the text above by volume and page number.

22. D. C. Somervell, *English Thought in the Nineteenth Century* (New York, 1929), pp. 10–11.

23. In an 1893 letter to Henry James, Stevenson asked, "How to get over, how to escape from, the besotting *particularity* of fiction. 'Roland approached the house; it had green doors and window blinds; and there was a scraper on the upper step.' To hell with Roland and the scraper."

24. See Thomas H. Johnson's "Jonathan Edwards," in *The Literary History of the United States: History,* ed. Robert E. Spiller *et al.* (New York and London, 1963).

25. See Kenneth Graham, *English Criticism of the Novel, 1865–1900,* pp. 112–13.

26. *George Eliot: Middlemarch* (Great Neck, N.Y., 1963), p. 9.

27. Annan, p. 271.

28. *English Literature and Society in the Eighteenth Century* (New York, 1962), p. 3. Subsequent citations from this edition are by page number in the text above.

Selected Bibliography

PRIMARY SOURCES

Multiple editions of a single title are cited where no single edition includes all essays. I have sometimes cited recently published editions in preference to first editions because of their accessibility.

I have included none of Stephen's many periodical essays, but most of the key Stephen essays are cited in my notes. See S. O. A. Ullmann's collection of Stephen's essays, *Men, Books, and Mountains: Essays by Leslie Stephen* (Minneapolis, Minn., 1956), for the fullest available Stephen bibliography.

An Agnostic's Apology and Other Essays. London: Smith, Elder, 1893.
Alexander Pope. English Men of Letters. London: Macmillan, 1880.
English Literature and Society in the Eighteenth Century. New York: Barnes and Noble, 1962.
The English Utilitarians. New York: Peter Smith, 1950.
Essays on Freethinking and Plainspeaking. London: Longmans, Green, 1873.
George Eliot. English Men of Letters. London: Macmillan, 1902.
The History of English Thought in the Eighteenth Century. 2 vols. New York: Harcourt, Brace and World, 1962.
Hobbes. English Men of Letters. Ann Arbor, Mich.: University of Michigan Press, 1961.
Hours in a Library. First and Second Series. 4 vols. London: Smith, Elder, 1892.
Life of Henry Fawcett. London: Smith, Elder, 1885.
Life of Sir James Fitzjames Stephen. London: Smith, Elder, 1895.
The Playground of Europe. London: Longmans, 1871.
The Playground of Europe, ed. H. E. G. Tyndale. Blackwell's Mountaineering Library. Oxford: Basil Blackwell, 1946.
Samuel Johnson. English Men of Letters. London: Macmillan, 1878.
The Science of Ethics. London: G. P. Putnam's Sons, 1882.
Sketches from Cambridge by a Don. London: Oxford U. Press, 1932.

Studies of a Biographer. [collected edition] 4 vols. New York and London: G. P. Putnam's Sons, 1907.
Swift. English Men of Letters. London: Macmillan, 1882.

SECONDARY SOURCES

This selective list contains only the most important studies of Stephen. Additional references of interest are contained in the notes.

ANNAN, NOEL G. Leslie Stephen: His Thought and Character in Relation to His Time. Cambridge, Mass.: Harvard University Press, 1952. This most important modern study of Stephen places him among Victorian middle-class intellectuals, a group which developed as a new aristocracy.

BICKNELL, JOHN. "Leslie Stephen as an Intellectual Historian." Unpublished doctoral dissertation, Cornell University, 1950. Assessment of Stephen's place in the development of the history of ideas.

COCKSHUT, A. O. J. The Unbelievers: English Agnostic Thought 1840–1890. London: Collins, 1964. Survey of liberal thought which suggests the general intellectual context of Stephen's agnosticism.

MAITLAND, FREDERIC W. The Life and Letters of Leslie Stephen. New York and London: G. P. Putnam's Sons, Duckworth, 1906. Basic published source for Stephen's life.

WILSON, JOHN D. Leslie Stephen and Matthew Arnold as Critics of Wordsworth. Cambridge, England: Cambridge University Press, 1939.

WOOLF, VIRGINIA. The Captain's Death Bed and Other Essays. New York: Harcourt, Brace, 1950. Stephen seen through the eyes of his most famous daughter.

The reader interested in all of the published sources of Stephen's biography would also want to see Quentin Bell's brief article "The Mausoleum Book," A Review of English Literature, VI (Jan., 1965), pp. 9–18.

Index

(The works of Leslie Stephen are listed under his name)

168